THE MAGIC MONEY JOURNAL

Published by Magic Money Books

Paperback ISBN: 978-1-947665-04-0

Digital ISBN: 978-1-947665-05-7

THIS JOURNAL BELONGS TO:

Name: ______________________________

Contact: ______________________________

Reward if found: $ __________

TABLE OF CONTENTS

MAGIC MONEY TIPS

Getting Started

To get the most out of *The Magic Money Journal,* please read through the Introduction and review the instructions for each Magic Money™ experiment.

Do What Works for You

The Introduction and instructions give you tried-and-true framework to get you started. Once you get into the flow of Magic Money™, be sure to keep going—and experiment with new ideas to see if they accelerate or increase your progress.

Keep it Simple, Light, and Fun!

Magic Money™ is *easy* and *fun*. You don't need to spend lots of time on it—just a few minutes a day will shift how you feel about money and allow it to come to you in magical ways.

Remember: abundance is everywhere and can come to you in unlimited amounts and at any time.

Begin Again

If you're like me, you'll need to begin again at least once (in my case, a half-dozen times). You can always have a new Day 1 and get amazing results within 24 hours.

Join Us!

Be sure to share what you're doing in the Magic Money Community on Facebook here:

http://Facebook.com/groups/MagicMoneyBooks

INTRODUCTION

Welcome to *The Magic Money Journal.* I'm excited to share it with you! This fourth and final installment in the series is a true amalgamation of my years of discovering, experimenting with, and polishing the Magic Money™ philosophy.

When I wrote the *Magic Money* book series, I encouraged the users to create a journal. It wasn't long before I got requests for examples of what I do in my own Magic Money™ journal. Some people wanted me to share an example of what I do in my journal's pages, most others just wanted me to create a journal they could use. This is a combination of both.

How to Use this Journal

There are a few aspects of a successful Magic Money™ practice I learned the hard way and can't recommend to you strongly enough. There is definitely an easier path and a harder path. I've spent a measurable amount of time on both, and believe me, easier is better. By a lot!

Get a Magic Money Buddy

I'm revising the saying "there's safety in numbers" to "there is strength in numbers." You can practice Magic Money™ in isolation and get along just fine. However, you may have times you want to bounce ideas off of someone who is on the same page. You might be frustrated because your progress is slower than you like, or you are getting the best results *ever* and want someone to share them with! Either way, a Magic Money™ buddy is a great idea. Not everyone has a best friend, significant other, or spouse who believe in Magic Money™ (I sure didn't), so connecting with someone who is doing their own Magic Money™ experiment (and it doesn't even need to be the same one you're doing) is a fine idea.

Tips for finding a buddy. Give a copy of *Beginning Magic Money* to a friend and encourage them to read it and do the first Magic Money™ experiment with you. Listen to the audiobook version on your daily commute and suggest someone you know and love do the same. There's no "right" buddy combination. We've got husband and wife, brother and sister, and mother and daughter Magic Money™ buddies already! You can also look for a buddy in the Magic Money Books Facebook group.

Put Your Magic Money Practice on Your Calendar

What gets scheduled gets attention, and your Magic Money™ practice is no different. Pull out your calendar and schedule time to write in *The Magic Money Journal* every day. Schedule time to say your mantras. You can say them in the car, shower, or even on your morning run. Write your favorites on 3 x 5" cards (you'll find some pre-printed cards to cut out in the back of this journal) and post them on the bathroom mirror, put them on your car's sun visor, and carry one in your wallet.

If You Stop, Start Again!

How many times did I stop and start again? I'm not tellin'! Seriously, I can't tell because it happened so often that I've lost count. I do know that if I hadn't restarted as many times as it took, I wouldn't have been able to figure it all out and share it with you. Even if you practice Magic Money™ faithfully for six months, you're on a roll and magnetizing money and abundance from the four corners of the Earth, you may for reasons you can't explain stop. And that's okay! It'll be here for you to pick back up again when you're ready.

I do remember the day I decided to do it until it became part of who I am—I had come face-to-face with another life challenge and the only thing I could do was speak, read, and write my mantras, intentions, and blessings. Everything felt completely out of control. I knew I wouldn't have to start over if I didn't stop in the first place! I committed to do the practice every single day, no matter what, even if I was (a) busy, (b) sick, (c) rich and abundant, or (d) trapped under something heavy (just seeing if you're paying attention). I kept adding it to my to-do list until practicing the Magic Money™ philosophy and writing in my journal wasn't an item on my to do list anymore. It had become part of who I am.

Ready, Set, Go!

The First 30-Day Experiment from Beginning Magic Money

You'll find the first 30-Day experiment on page 2. You'll just fill in the blank spaces every day, watch the magic happen, and record your result and observations.

Free Bonus: First 30-Day Experiment Download

If you're like many Magic Money™ practitioners, you may feel like another "First" 30-Day Experiment is in order. I understand! You'll find a printable PDF here: MagicMoneyBooks.com/FirstExp

Second 30-Day Experiment from Advanced Magic Money

In your Second 30-Day Experiment, you'll have the opportunity to allocate your money according to the Magic Money™ Philosophy. You'll put Magic Money™ Maximization into practice…and I think you're going to *love* it!

The Rest of the Year: Magic Money Mastery

Your final Magic Money™ experiment lasts as long as you want it to last (perhaps forever). You'll set a lifelong Magic Money™ intention, and then continue to "work the magic" for as long as you like.

RESOURCES

THE SEVEN MAGIC MONEY STEPS

Number One

Take control of what you think, say, and do with money.

Number Two

Suspend disbelief.

Number Three

Let go of every belief you have that money must come to you through specific channels (i.e., through your job/career, an individual or entity, etc.).

Number Four

Think and speak about money in a positive way.

Number Five

Allow money to come to you from anywhere at any time.

Number Six

Believe that there's more than enough for you now and henceforth forever.

Number Seven

Know an abundance of everything you need is indeed on its way to you *right now*.

Tips For Raising Your Vibration

The higher your vibration, the easier the manifestation. Having a high vibration can take effort, especially as you integrate the Magic Money™ philosophy into your daily life.

Here are a few ways I've discovered to raise my vibration when needed (and keep it high, no matter what):

- Re-read the book(s) and other resources.
- Post in the Magic Money Facebook community, and visit Joe Carlisle's Magic Money Project Facebook group.

- Listen to some amazing music. *Listen to upbeat, fun, or even inspiring music.*
- Say your affirmations, out loud, with passion! *I walk around my home, touch just about everything, and give thanks to it and for it for being in my life.*
- Go for a walk, a run, or do some other kind of workout. *Bonus points if you're outside in nature.*
- Watch something funny. Try a movie, a television series, or watch some kitten videos on YouTube.
- Eat something that makes you happy, and is nourishing for your body.
- Feng shui your home, car, office.

YOUR FIRST MAGIC MONEY EXPERIMENT

from *Beginning Magic Money*

First, choose the amount of money you want to provide for the person or organization of your choice. Then, continue with these four steps in your first experiment.

One. Take responsibility for your life and everything in it. You are not a victim. There is no one to blame for anything. The choices you've made up until now have brought you to where you are today, good, bad, or indifferent.

Ultimately, there is no good or bad—it just is. Accept every aspect of your life, including—and perhaps especially—your financial situation, just as it is.

Two. Stop complaining, bemoaning, or bellyaching. No more criticizing. Not even a tiny bit of gossiping, back-fence talking, or scuttlebutt. If you don't have anything nice to say, say nothing. If you're really having a tough day, or someone has been particularly mean to you, resist the urge to light them on fire and repeat (to yourself and anyone who asks how you are doing): "Everything is working out for my highest good, and I can't wait to see what happens next!"

Three. Keep a running list of everything you are grateful for, or could be grateful for, if you were paying closer attention (you'll find one in here, starting on page 32. You live in a world of massive abundance, and your job is to notice it, notate it, and be grateful for it. Make it a point to add to your gratitude list every day, at least once a day. Magic Money™ flows to the person who lives in a constant state of gratitude for gratitude is just another way to describe the state of abundance. Write down as many things down as you can every day.

Whenever you feel doubt, lack, or fear, write at least five things down. And walk around your home, touch the objects you own, and be thankful for them.

Bonus points: Write thank you notes!

Four. Watch for, and record, your results. Receive unexpected income for work you've done? Note that. Get a new client or customer "out of the blue?" Put it on the list. An unexpected check arrives in the mail? Write it down. You find money on the sidewalk? Yup, that's not only a positive result, it is a sign you are on the right track. It is the Universe giving you a wink. Nod, smile to yourself, and write it in *The Magic Money Journal.*

That's it. That's your first Magic Money™ experiment. At the end of 30 days, you should have a notebook full of things you're grateful for, and Magic Money™ manifestations. If you can last to at least sixty or ninety days, you'll probably have used up more than one journal!

I, ______________________________, take responsibility for my life and everything in it for the duration of this experiment (and beyond)!

I, ______________________________, will stop complaining, bemoaning, or bellyaching. I won't criticize, gossip, back-fence talk, or discuss scuttle-butt. If I don't have anything nice to say, I will say nothing. If I'm having a really tough day, or someone has been particularly mean to me, I will resist the urge to light them on fire and repeat (to myself and anyone who asks how I am): "Everything is working out for my highest good, and I can't wait to see what happens next!"

I am grateful for:

____

____

____

____

____

____

____

____

I wrote thank you notes to: ______________________________

____

My results (magical things that happened, abundance I noticed, money I was given, received, or found):

____

____

____

____

____

____

____

____

____

DATE:	$	MAGIC MONEY DAY 2

I take responsibility for my life and everything in it for the duration of this experiment (and beyond)!

I will stop complaining, bemoaning, or bellyaching. I won't criticize, gossip, back-fence talk, or discuss scuttle-butt. If I don't have anything nice to say, I will say nothing. If I'm having a really tough day, or someone has been particularly mean to me, I will resist the urge to light them on fire and repeat (to myself and anyone who asks how I am doing): "Everything is working out for my highest good, and I can't wait to see what happens next!"

I am grateful for:

I wrote thank you notes to:

My results (magical things that happened, abundance I noticed, money I was given, received, or found):

I take responsibility for my life and everything in it for the duration of this experiment (and beyond)!

I will stop complaining, bemoaning, or bellyaching. I won't criticize, gossip, back-fence talk, or discuss scuttle-butt. If I don't have anything nice to say, I will say nothing. If I'm having a really tough day, or someone has been particularly mean to me, I will resist the urge to light them on fire and repeat (to myself and anyone who asks how I am doing): "Everything is working out for my highest good, and I can't wait to see what happens next!"

I am grateful for:

I wrote thank you notes to:

My results (magical things that happened, abundance I noticed, money I was given, received, or found):

I take responsibility for my life and everything in it for the duration of this experiment (and beyond)!

I will stop complaining, bemoaning, or bellyaching. I won't criticize, gossip, back-fence talk, or discuss scuttle-butt. If I don't have anything nice to say, I will say nothing. If I'm having a really tough day, or someone has been particularly mean to me, I will resist the urge to light them on fire and repeat (to myself and anyone who asks how I am doing): "Everything is working out for my highest good, and I can't wait to see what happens next!"

I am grateful for:

I wrote thank you notes to:

My results (magical things that happened, abundance I noticed, money I was given, received, or found):

DATE:	$	MAGIC MONEY DAY 5

I take responsibility for my life and everything in it for the duration of this experiment (and beyond)!

I will stop complaining, bemoaning, or bellyaching. I won't criticize, gossip, back-fence talk, or discuss scuttle-butt. If I don't have anything nice to say, I will say nothing. If I'm having a really tough day, or someone has been particularly mean to me, I will resist the urge to light them on fire and repeat (to myself and anyone who asks how I am doing): "Everything is working out for my highest good, and I can't wait to see what happens next!"

I am grateful for:

____

____

____

____

____

____

____

____

I wrote thank you notes to: ____________________________

____

My results (magical things that happened, abundance I noticed, money I was given, received, or found):

____

____

____

____

____

____

____

____

____

____

____

DATE:	$	MAGIC MONEY DAY 6

I take responsibility for my life and everything in it for the duration of this experiment (and beyond)!

I will stop complaining, bemoaning, or bellyaching. I won't criticize, gossip, back-fence talk, or discuss scuttle-butt. If I don't have anything nice to say, I will say nothing. If I'm having a really tough day, or someone has been particularly mean to me, I will resist the urge to light them on fire and repeat (to myself and anyone who asks how I am doing): "Everything is working out for my highest good, and I can't wait to see what happens next!"

I am grateful for:

I wrote thank you notes to:

My results (magical things that happened, abundance I noticed, money I was given, received, or found):

DATE: $ MAGIC MONEY DAY 7

I take responsibility for my life and everything in it for the duration of this experiment (and beyond)!

I will stop complaining, bemoaning, or bellyaching. I won't criticize, gossip, back-fence talk, or discuss scuttle-butt. If I don't have anything nice to say, I will say nothing. If I'm having a really tough day, or someone has been particularly mean to me, I will resist the urge to light them on fire and repeat (to myself and anyone who asks how I am doing): "Everything is working out for my highest good, and I can't wait to see what happens next!"

I am grateful for:

____

____

____

____

____

____

____

____

I wrote thank you notes to: ____

____

My results (magical things that happened, abundance I noticed, money I was given, received, or found):

____

____

____

____

____

____

____

____

____

____

____

DATE:	$	MAGIC MONEY DAY 8

I take responsibility for my life and everything in it for the duration of this experiment (and beyond)!

I will stop complaining, bemoaning, or bellyaching. I won't criticize, gossip, back-fence talk, or discuss scuttle-butt. If I don't have anything nice to say, I will say nothing. If I'm having a really tough day, or someone has been particularly mean to me, I will resist the urge to light them on fire and repeat (to myself and anyone who asks how I am doing): "Everything is working out for my highest good, and I can't wait to see what happens next!"

I am grateful for:

I wrote thank you notes to:

My results (magical things that happened, abundance I noticed, money I was given, received, or found):

I take responsibility for my life and everything in it for the duration of this experiment (and beyond)!

I will stop complaining, bemoaning, or bellyaching. I won't criticize, gossip, back-fence talk, or discuss scuttle-butt. If I don't have anything nice to say, I will say nothing. If I'm having a really tough day, or someone has been particularly mean to me, I will resist the urge to light them on fire and repeat (to myself and anyone who asks how I am doing): "Everything is working out for my highest good, and I can't wait to see what happens next!"

I am grateful for:

I wrote thank you notes to:

My results (magical things that happened, abundance I noticed, money I was given, received, or found):

I take responsibility for my life and everything in it for the duration of this experiment (and beyond)!

I will stop complaining, bemoaning, or bellyaching. I won't criticize, gossip, back-fence talk, or discuss scuttle-butt. If I don't have anything nice to say, I will say nothing. If I'm having a really tough day, or someone has been particularly mean to me, I will resist the urge to light them on fire and repeat (to myself and anyone who asks how I am doing): "Everything is working out for my highest good, and I can't wait to see what happens next!"

I am grateful for:

I wrote thank you notes to:

My results (magical things that happened, abundance I noticed, money I was given, received, or found):

DATE:	$	MAGIC MONEY DAY 11

I take responsibility for my life and everything in it for the duration of this experiment (and beyond)!

I will stop complaining, bemoaning, or bellyaching. I won't criticize, gossip, back-fence talk, or discuss scuttle-butt. If I don't have anything nice to say, I will say nothing. If I'm having a really tough day, or someone has been particularly mean to me, I will resist the urge to light them on fire and repeat (to myself and anyone who asks how I am doing): "Everything is working out for my highest good, and I can't wait to see what happens next!"

I am grateful for:

I wrote thank you notes to:

My results (magical things that happened, abundance I noticed, money I was given, received, or found):

I take responsibility for my life and everything in it for the duration of this experiment (and beyond)!

I will stop complaining, bemoaning, or bellyaching. I won't criticize, gossip, back-fence talk, or discuss scuttle-butt. If I don't have anything nice to say, I will say nothing. If I'm having a really tough day, or someone has been particularly mean to me, I will resist the urge to light them on fire and repeat (to myself and anyone who asks how I am doing): "Everything is working out for my highest good, and I can't wait to see what happens next!"

I am grateful for:

I wrote thank you notes to:

My results (magical things that happened, abundance I noticed, money I was given, received, or found):

DATE:	$	MAGIC MONEY DAY 13

I take responsibility for my life and everything in it for the duration of this experiment (and beyond)!

I will stop complaining, bemoaning, or bellyaching. I won't criticize, gossip, back-fence talk, or discuss scuttle-butt. If I don't have anything nice to say, I will say nothing. If I'm having a really tough day, or someone has been particularly mean to me, I will resist the urge to light them on fire and repeat (to myself and anyone who asks how I am doing): "Everything is working out for my highest good, and I can't wait to see what happens next!"

I am grateful for:

I wrote thank you notes to:

My results (magical things that happened, abundance I noticed, money I was given, received, or found):

I take responsibility for my life and everything in it for the duration of this experiment (and beyond)!

I will stop complaining, bemoaning, or bellyaching. I won't criticize, gossip, back-fence talk, or discuss scuttle-butt. If I don't have anything nice to say, I will say nothing. If I'm having a really tough day, or someone has been particularly mean to me, I will resist the urge to light them on fire and repeat (to myself and anyone who asks how I am doing): "Everything is working out for my highest good, and I can't wait to see what happens next!"

I am grateful for:

I wrote thank you notes to:

My results (magical things that happened, abundance I noticed, money I was given, received, or found):

I take responsibility for my life and everything in it for the duration of this experiment (and beyond)!

I will stop complaining, bemoaning, or bellyaching. I won't criticize, gossip, back-fence talk, or discuss scuttle-butt. If I don't have anything nice to say, I will say nothing. If I'm having a really tough day, or someone has been particularly mean to me, I will resist the urge to light them on fire and repeat (to myself and anyone who asks how I am doing): "Everything is working out for my highest good, and I can't wait to see what happens next!"

I am grateful for:

I wrote thank you notes to:

My results (magical things that happened, abundance I noticed, money I was given, received, or found):

I take responsibility for my life and everything in it for the duration of this experiment (and beyond)!

I will stop complaining, bemoaning, or bellyaching. I won't criticize, gossip, back-fence talk, or discuss scuttle-butt. If I don't have anything nice to say, I will say nothing. If I'm having a really tough day, or someone has been particularly mean to me, I will resist the urge to light them on fire and repeat (to myself and anyone who asks how I am doing): "Everything is working out for my highest good, and I can't wait to see what happens next!"

I am grateful for:

I wrote thank you notes to:

My results (magical things that happened, abundance I noticed, money I was given, received, or found):

I take responsibility for my life and everything in it for the duration of this experiment (and beyond)!

I will stop complaining, bemoaning, or bellyaching. I won't criticize, gossip, back-fence talk, or discuss scuttle-butt. If I don't have anything nice to say, I will say nothing. If I'm having a really tough day, or someone has been particularly mean to me, I will resist the urge to light them on fire and repeat (to myself and anyone who asks how I am doing): "Everything is working out for my highest good, and I can't wait to see what happens next!"

I am grateful for:

I wrote thank you notes to:

My results (magical things that happened, abundance I noticed, money I was given, received, or found):

I take responsibility for my life and everything in it for the duration of this experiment (and beyond)!

I will stop complaining, bemoaning, or bellyaching. I won't criticize, gossip, back-fence talk, or discuss scuttle-butt. If I don't have anything nice to say, I will say nothing. If I'm having a really tough day, or someone has been particularly mean to me, I will resist the urge to light them on fire and repeat (to myself and anyone who asks how I am doing): "Everything is working out for my highest good, and I can't wait to see what happens next!"

I am grateful for:

I wrote thank you notes to:

My results (magical things that happened, abundance I noticed, money I was given, received, or found):

DATE:	$	MAGIC MONEY DAY 19

I take responsibility for my life and everything in it for the duration of this experiment (and beyond)!

I will stop complaining, bemoaning, or bellyaching. I won't criticize, gossip, back-fence talk, or discuss scuttle-butt. If I don't have anything nice to say, I will say nothing. If I'm having a really tough day, or someone has been particularly mean to me, I will resist the urge to light them on fire and repeat (to myself and anyone who asks how I am doing): "Everything is working out for my highest good, and I can't wait to see what happens next!"

I am grateful for:

I wrote thank you notes to:

My results (magical things that happened, abundance I noticed, money I was given, received, or found):

I take responsibility for my life and everything in it for the duration of this experiment (and beyond)!

I will stop complaining, bemoaning, or bellyaching. I won't criticize, gossip, back-fence talk, or discuss scuttle-butt. If I don't have anything nice to say, I will say nothing. If I'm having a really tough day, or someone has been particularly mean to me, I will resist the urge to light them on fire and repeat (to myself and anyone who asks how I am doing): "Everything is working out for my highest good, and I can't wait to see what happens next!"

I am grateful for:

I wrote thank you notes to:

My results (magical things that happened, abundance I noticed, money I was given, received, or found):

I take responsibility for my life and everything in it for the duration of this experiment (and beyond)!

I will stop complaining, bemoaning, or bellyaching. I won't criticize, gossip, back-fence talk, or discuss scuttle-butt. If I don't have anything nice to say, I will say nothing. If I'm having a really tough day, or someone has been particularly mean to me, I will resist the urge to light them on fire and repeat (to myself and anyone who asks how I am doing): "Everything is working out for my highest good, and I can't wait to see what happens next!"

I am grateful for:

I wrote thank you notes to:

My results (magical things that happened, abundance I noticed, money I was given, received, or found):

I take responsibility for my life and everything in it for the duration of this experiment (and beyond)!

I will stop complaining, bemoaning, or bellyaching. I won't criticize, gossip, back-fence talk, or discuss scuttle-butt. If I don't have anything nice to say, I will say nothing. If I'm having a really tough day, or someone has been particularly mean to me, I will resist the urge to light them on fire and repeat (to myself and anyone who asks how I am doing): "Everything is working out for my highest good, and I can't wait to see what happens next!"

I am grateful for:

I wrote thank you notes to:

My results (magical things that happened, abundance I noticed, money I was given, received, or found):

I take responsibility for my life and everything in it for the duration of this experiment (and beyond)!

I will stop complaining, bemoaning, or bellyaching. I won't criticize, gossip, back-fence talk, or discuss scuttle-butt. If I don't have anything nice to say, I will say nothing. If I'm having a really tough day, or someone has been particularly mean to me, I will resist the urge to light them on fire and repeat (to myself and anyone who asks how I am doing): "Everything is working out for my highest good, and I can't wait to see what happens next!"

I am grateful for:

I wrote thank you notes to:

My results (magical things that happened, abundance I noticed, money I was given, received, or found):

DATE:	$	MAGIC MONEY DAY 24

I take responsibility for my life and everything in it for the duration of this experiment (and beyond)!

I will stop complaining, bemoaning, or bellyaching. I won't criticize, gossip, back-fence talk, or discuss scuttle-butt. If I don't have anything nice to say, I will say nothing. If I'm having a really tough day, or someone has been particularly mean to me, I will resist the urge to light them on fire and repeat (to myself and anyone who asks how I am doing): "Everything is working out for my highest good, and I can't wait to see what happens next!"

I am grateful for:

I wrote thank you notes to:

My results (magical things that happened, abundance I noticed, money I was given, received, or found):

I take responsibility for my life and everything in it for the duration of this experiment (and beyond)!

I will stop complaining, bemoaning, or bellyaching. I won't criticize, gossip, back-fence talk, or discuss scuttle-butt. If I don't have anything nice to say, I will say nothing. If I'm having a really tough day, or someone has been particularly mean to me, I will resist the urge to light them on fire and repeat (to myself and anyone who asks how I am doing): "Everything is working out for my highest good, and I can't wait to see what happens next!"

I am grateful for:

I wrote thank you notes to:

My results (magical things that happened, abundance I noticed, money I was given, received, or found):

I take responsibility for my life and everything in it for the duration of this experiment (and beyond)!

I will stop complaining, bemoaning, or bellyaching. I won't criticize, gossip, back-fence talk, or discuss scuttle-butt. If I don't have anything nice to say, I will say nothing. If I'm having a really tough day, or someone has been particularly mean to me, I will resist the urge to light them on fire and repeat (to myself and anyone who asks how I am doing): "Everything is working out for my highest good, and I can't wait to see what happens next!"

I am grateful for:

I wrote thank you notes to:

My results (magical things that happened, abundance I noticed, money I was given, received, or found):

I take responsibility for my life and everything in it for the duration of this experiment (and beyond)!

I will stop complaining, bemoaning, or bellyaching. I won't criticize, gossip, back-fence talk, or discuss scuttle-butt. If I don't have anything nice to say, I will say nothing. If I'm having a really tough day, or someone has been particularly mean to me, I will resist the urge to light them on fire and repeat (to myself and anyone who asks how I am doing): "Everything is working out for my highest good, and I can't wait to see what happens next!"

I am grateful for:

I wrote thank you notes to:

My results (magical things that happened, abundance I noticed, money I was given, received, or found):

DATE: $ MAGIC MONEY DAY 28

I take responsibility for my life and everything in it for the duration of this experiment (and beyond)!

I will stop complaining, bemoaning, or bellyaching. I won't criticize, gossip, back-fence talk, or discuss scuttle-butt. If I don't have anything nice to say, I will say nothing. If I'm having a really tough day, or someone has been particularly mean to me, I will resist the urge to light them on fire and repeat (to myself and anyone who asks how I am doing): "Everything is working out for my highest good, and I can't wait to see what happens next!"

I am grateful for:

I wrote thank you notes to:

My results (magical things that happened, abundance I noticed, money I was given, received, or found):

I take responsibility for my life and everything in it for the duration of this experiment (and beyond)!

I will stop complaining, bemoaning, or bellyaching. I won't criticize, gossip, back-fence talk, or discuss scuttle-butt. If I don't have anything nice to say, I will say nothing. If I'm having a really tough day, or someone has been particularly mean to me, I will resist the urge to light them on fire and repeat (to myself and anyone who asks how I am doing): "Everything is working out for my highest good, and I can't wait to see what happens next!"

I am grateful for:

I wrote thank you notes to:

My results (magical things that happened, abundance I noticed, money I was given, received, or found):

DATE:	$	MAGIC MONEY DAY 30

I take responsibility for my life and everything in it for the duration of this experiment (and beyond)!

I will stop complaining, bemoaning, or bellyaching. I won't criticize, gossip, back-fence talk, or discuss scuttle-butt. If I don't have anything nice to say, I will say nothing. If I'm having a really tough day, or someone has been particularly mean to me, I will resist the urge to light them on fire and repeat (to myself and anyone who asks how I am doing): "Everything is working out for my highest good, and I can't wait to see what happens next!"

I am grateful for:

I wrote thank you notes to:

My results (magical things that happened, abundance I noticed, money I was given, received, or found):

MY GRATITUDE LIST

This is a list of everything and everyone in my life I am grateful for:

YOUR SECOND MAGIC MONEY EXPERIMENT

from *Advanced Magic Money*

Let's review the guidelines of your first Magic Money™ experiment from *Beginning Magic Money* because they still (and will always) apply:

One. Take responsibility for your life and everything in it.

Two. Stop complaining, moaning, or bellyaching.

Three. Keep a running gratitude list.

Four. Watch for and record, your results (money, clients, goods, services, discounts, found money, etc.).

Keep engaging the magic by continuing these practices until—*until forever.* Make them daily habits you practice.

Now, let's add some new actions for this next experiment. Mark your calendar for 30 days from today, and get ready to do the following:

One. My Master Manifestation List.

I've saved the first four pages for you to write your master list of every thing, situation, and event you want to manifest into your life, now and in the future. You set your intentions *in writing.*

Write everything you can think of right now, and return to this list to add more as they occur to you.

If you have an outstanding medical bill you can't quite pay today, write *I easily paid the $2,836 bill to ABC Medical Services*. Want to gain or lose some weight? Try *I now weigh 185 lbs., am in the best shape and health of my life, and feel terrific every single day.* What's that? You've been yearning to take an Alaskan cruise? Easy like Sunday morning: *I had the best time on the 10-day Glacier Bay Alaskan cruise aboard the Norwegian Jewel. Alaska was breathtaking, and I can't believe how much I ate!*

Yup, you guessed it, you write your master list as though everything on it has already come to fruition.

Two. Write today's date at the top of each page.

Underneath the date, write *It is so amazing that …* and, one line at a time, write down what you want to happen today as though it has already happened. Let me share a few examples:

- Mark is respectful and cleans his room without a reminder.
- I engaged Bob Smith as a new client, I received his signed contract, and he paid in full for one year.
- My annual review was great, and I received an 18% raise and $125,000 bonus.
- The car wash was empty, and I was in and out in twenty minutes!
- My workout was amazing, and I am stronger and faster than ever!

Look at your day, see what's on your calendar, then picture the day as already done. Imagine yourself at the end of the day today, and everything went perfectly. A pitch meeting with a prospective client? They say "yes!" and are excited to work with you. Are your kids bringing home their report cards? They arrive home, with all As, of course, and you have a celebratory dinner at their favorite restaurant. Taking your car in for the 120,000-mile checkup? Magically, it's in terrific shape and only needs a simple oil change. Expecting a signed contract or check in the mail? Yup, it arrives on (or ahead of) schedule.

It's your job to picture each item on your list as done, to envision each activity as though it has happened perfectly. You're setting your intentions *with visualization.*

Three. Speak Magic Money.

While Magic Money™ isn't an official language, you do need to learn the new language of Magic Money™ to attract it!

This part of your second Magic Money™ experiment is multi-faceted:

- Speak about things only as you want them to be.
- *Cancel* any words you utter that are contrary to what you want.
- Remain unmoved when you see things moving in the wrong direction, or even results you don't want.
- Remain unattached to your outcomes.
- Ask yourself the Positive Power Questions (PPQs).
- Bless everything and everyone as good.

Remember: everything that happens is a sign of awesomeness!

When you ask for something, always add *this or something better.*

Four. Practice Magic Money Maximization.

If you haven't already, decide what percentage of all monies you receive, you're going to use to practice Magic Money™ maximization.

When you receive money (i.e., the day it's officially cleared your bank account for use, or you have the cold hard cash in your hands), do the following:

- Give x% away.
- Save x%.
- Use x% to pay off your debt.
- Set aside x% for taxes.
- Put x% in your fun account. If you can, have fun *right away!*

You might be tempted to wait until tomorrow, or the weekend, or sometime later to distribute your money. Please do it *as soon as possible.* The sooner you allocate your money, the sooner the Universe will say *Aha! She's serious! My turn to act!*

Ideally, you'll start with or increase your distributions to 10% (or more!) over time. If you are in a time of financial struggle, keep in mind the tide can turn immediately and you can absolutely find yourself flush with abundance quick as a flash!

Your intentional and timely money management will serve you in at least two ways: you will feel good and full of confidence about taking control of your money, and you will set magical and invisible forces in motion to work on your behalf.

Remember, even beginning with just 1% will fully engage Magic Money™ and the Universe will begin working on your behalf immediately. Remember with your first Magic Money™ experiment how you experienced something incredible within the first 24 hours? Don't be surprised when something amazing happens.

You may notice how abundant you feel. Or, you might feel a tightness in your chest. You might be skeptical. Wherever you are on the emotional money scale is perfectly normal. Follow the steps. Review them. Commit them to memory. Take the action you're inspired to take. Record your results.

Spend at least 30 days allocating your money according to the Magic Money™ philosophy, and I'm sure by the end of the 30th day, you will be hooked!

MY MASTER MANIFESTATION LIST

What I want to manifest, even though I have *no idea* how it could possibly happen:

Today I'm feeling ______________________________

____

The exciting things I have in store for today are ______________________________

____

Today's Magic Money™ mantra is ______________________________

____

Today's Magic Money™ intention(s): It is so amazing that...

____

____

____

I bless ______________________________

______________________________ *as good, good, good!*

Today's Magic Money™ results include:

____

____

____

These magical things happened today...

____

____

____

☐ I practiced **Magic Money™ maximization** today, and gave ____ %/$ to ________________ saved ____ %/$ in my opportunity chest, paid ____ %/$ for debt, put aside ____ %/$ for taxes and saved ____ %/$ for fun! It's going to be so fun to ______________________________.

Today I'm feeling ______________________________

____

The exciting things I have in store for today are ______________________________

____

Today's Magic Money™ mantra is ______________________________

____

Today's Magic Money™ intention(s): It is so amazing that…

____

____

____

I bless ______________________________

______________________________ *as good, good, good!*

Today's Magic Money™ results include:

____

____

____

These magical things happened today…

____

____

____

☐ I practiced **Magic Money™ maximization** today, and gave ____ %/$ to ________________ saved ____ %/$ in my opportunity chest, paid ____ %/$ for debt, put aside ____ %/$ for taxes and saved ____ %/$ for fun! It's going to be so fun to ______________________________.

Today I'm feeling ______________________________

____

The exciting things I have in store for today are ______________________________

____

Today's Magic Money™ mantra is ______________________________

____

Today's Magic Money™ intention(s): It is so amazing that…

____

____

____

I bless ______________________________

______________________________ *as good, good, good!*

Today's Magic Money™ results include:

____

____

____

These magical things happened today…

____

____

____

☐ I practiced **Magic Money™ maximization** today, and gave ____ %/$ to ________________ saved ____ %/$ in my opportunity chest, paid ____ %/$ for debt, put aside ____ %/$ for taxes and saved ____ %/$ for fun! It's going to be so fun to ______________________________.

DATE: $ MAGIC MONEY DAY 34

Today I'm feeling ______________________________

____

The exciting things I have in store for today are ______________________________

____

Today's Magic Money™ mantra is ______________________________

____

Today's Magic Money™ intention(s): It is so amazing that…

____

____

____

I bless ______________________________

______________________________ *as good, good, good!*

Today's Magic Money™ results include:

____

____

____

These magical things happened today…

____

____

____

☐ I practiced **Magic Money™ maximization** today, and gave ____ %/$ to ________________ saved ____ %/$ in my opportunity chest, paid ____ %/$ for debt, put aside ____ %/$ for taxes and saved ____ %/$ for fun! It's going to be so fun to ______________________________.

Today I'm feeling ______________________________

____

The exciting things I have in store for today are ______________________________

____

Today's Magic Money™ mantra is ______________________________

____

Today's Magic Money™ intention(s): It is so amazing that...

____

____

____

I bless ______________________________

______________________________ *as good, good, good!*

Today's Magic Money™ results include:

____

____

____

These magical things happened today...

____

____

____

☐ I practiced **Magic Money™ maximization** today, and gave ____ %/$ to __________________ saved ____ %/$ in my opportunity chest, paid ____ %/$ for debt, put aside ____ %/$ for taxes and saved ____ %/$ for fun! It's going to be so fun to ______________________________.

DATE: **$** **MAGIC MONEY DAY 36**

Today I'm feeling ______________________________

____

The exciting things I have in store for today are ______________________________

____

Today's Magic Money™ mantra is ______________________________

____

Today's Magic Money™ intention(s): It is so amazing that…

____

____

____

I bless ______________________________

______________________________ *as good, good, good!*

Today's Magic Money™ results include:

____

____

____

These magical things happened today…

____

____

____

☐ I practiced **Magic Money™ maximization** today, and gave ____ %/$ to ________________ saved ____ %/$ in my opportunity chest, paid ____ %/$ for debt, put aside ____ %/$ for taxes and saved ____ %/$ for fun! It's going to be so fun to ______________________________.

Today I'm feeling ______________________________

____

The exciting things I have in store for today are ______________________________

____

Today's Magic Money™ mantra is ______________________________

____

Today's Magic Money™ intention(s): It is so amazing that…

____

____

____

I bless ______________________________

______________________________ *as good, good, good!*

Today's Magic Money™ results include:

____

____

____

These magical things happened today…

____

____

____

☐ I practiced **Magic Money™ maximization** today, and gave ____ %/$ to ______________ saved ____ %/$ in my opportunity chest, paid ____ %/$ for debt, put aside ____ %/$ for taxes and saved ____ %/$ for fun! It's going to be so fun to ______________________________.

Today I'm feeling ______________________________

____

The exciting things I have in store for today are ______________________________

____

Today's Magic Money™ mantra is ______________________________

____

Today's Magic Money™ intention(s): It is so amazing that…

____

____

____

I bless ______________________________

______________________________ *as good, good, good!*

Today's Magic Money™ results include:

____

____

____

These magical things happened today…

____

____

____

☐ I practiced **Magic Money™ maximization** today, and gave ____ %/$ to ________________ saved ____ %/$ in my opportunity chest, paid ____ %/$ for debt, put aside ____ %/$ for taxes and saved ____ %/$ for fun! It's going to be so fun to ______________________________.

Today I'm feeling ______________________________

____

The exciting things I have in store for today are ______________________________

____

Today's Magic Money™ mantra is ______________________________

____

Today's Magic Money™ intention(s): It is so amazing that…

____

____

____

I bless ______________________________

______________________________ *as good, good, good!*

Today's Magic Money™ results include:

____

____

____

These magical things happened today…

____

____

____

☐ I practiced **Magic Money™ maximization** today, and gave ____ %/$ to ________________ saved ____ %/$ in my opportunity chest, paid ____ %/$ for debt, put aside ____ %/$ for taxes and saved ____ %/$ for fun! It's going to be so fun to ______________________________.

DATE:	$	MAGIC MONEY DAY 40

Today I'm feeling ______________________________

____

The exciting things I have in store for today are ______________________________

____

Today's Magic Money™ mantra is ______________________________

____

Today's Magic Money™ intention(s): It is so amazing that...

____

____

____

I bless ______________________________

______________________________ *as good, good, good!*

Today's Magic Money™ results include:

____

____

____

These magical things happened today...

____

____

____

☐ I practiced **Magic Money™ maximization** today, and gave ____ %/$ to ________________ saved ____ %/$ in my opportunity chest, paid ____ %/$ for debt, put aside ____ %/$ for taxes and saved ____ %/$ for fun! It's going to be so fun to ______________________________.

Today I'm feeling ______________________________

____

The exciting things I have in store for today are ______________________________

____

Today's Magic Money™ mantra is ______________________________

____

Today's Magic Money™ intention(s): It is so amazing that…

____

____

____

I bless ______________________________

______________________________ *as good, good, good!*

Today's Magic Money™ results include:

____

____

____

These magical things happened today…

____

____

____

☐ I practiced **Magic Money™ maximization** today, and gave ____ %/$ to ________________ saved ____ %/$ in my opportunity chest, paid ____ %/$ for debt, put aside ____ %/$ for taxes and saved ____ %/$ for fun! It's going to be so fun to ______________________________.

Today I'm feeling ______________________________

____

The exciting things I have in store for today are ______________________________

____

Today's Magic Money™ mantra is ______________________________

____

Today's Magic Money™ intention(s): It is so amazing that…

____

____

____

I bless ______________________________

______________________________*as good, good, good!*

Today's Magic Money™ results include:

____

____

____

These magical things happened today…

____

____

____

☐ I practiced **Magic Money™ maximization** today, and gave ____ %/$ to ________________ saved ____ %/$ in my opportunity chest, paid ____ %/$ for debt, put aside ____ %/$ for taxes and saved ____ %/$ for fun! It's going to be so fun to ______________________________.

Today I'm feeling ______________________________

____

The exciting things I have in store for today are ______________________________

____

Today's Magic Money™ mantra is ______________________________

____

Today's Magic Money™ intention(s): It is so amazing that…

____

____

____

I bless ______________________________

______________________________ *as good, good, good!*

Today's Magic Money™ results include:

____

____

____

These magical things happened today…

____

____

____

☐ I practiced **Magic Money™ maximization** today, and gave ____ %/$ to ________________ saved ____ %/$ in my opportunity chest, paid ____ %/$ for debt, put aside ____ %/$ for taxes and saved ____ %/$ for fun! It's going to be so fun to ______________________________.

Today I'm feeling ______________________________

____

The exciting things I have in store for today are ______________________________

____

Today's Magic Money™ mantra is ______________________________

____

Today's Magic Money™ intention(s): It is so amazing that…

____

____

____

I bless ______________________________

______________________________*as good, good, good!*

Today's Magic Money™ results include:

____

____

____

These magical things happened today…

____

____

____

☐ I practiced **Magic Money™ maximization** today, and gave ____ %/$ to ________________ saved ____ %/$ in my opportunity chest, paid ____ %/$ for debt, put aside ____ %/$ for taxes and saved ____ %/$ for fun! It's going to be so fun to ______________________________.

Today I'm feeling ______________________________

____

The exciting things I have in store for today are ______________________________

____

Today's Magic Money™ mantra is ______________________________

____

Today's Magic Money™ intention(s): It is so amazing that…

____

____

____

I bless ______________________________

______________________________ *as good, good, good!*

Today's Magic Money™ results include:

____

____

____

These magical things happened today…

____

____

____

☐ I practiced **Magic Money™ maximization** today, and gave ____ %/$ to ________________ saved ____ %/$ in my opportunity chest, paid ____ %/$ for debt, put aside ____ %/$ for taxes and saved ____ %/$ for fun! It's going to be so fun to ______________________________.

Today I'm feeling ______________________________

____

The exciting things I have in store for today are ______________________________

____

Today's Magic Money™ mantra is ______________________________

____

Today's Magic Money™ intention(s): It is so amazing that…

____

____

____

I bless ______________________________

______________________________ *as good, good, good!*

Today's Magic Money™ results include:

____

____

____

These magical things happened today…

____

____

____

☐ I practiced **Magic Money™ maximization** today, and gave ____ %/$ to ________________ saved ____ %/$ in my opportunity chest, paid ____ %/$ for debt, put aside ____ %/$ for taxes and saved ____ %/$ for fun! It's going to be so fun to ______________________________.

Today I'm feeling ______________________________

____

The exciting things I have in store for today are ______________________________

____

Today's Magic Money™ mantra is ______________________________

____

Today's Magic Money™ intention(s): It is so amazing that…

____

____

____

I bless ______________________________

______________________________ ***as good, good, good!***

Today's Magic Money™ results include:

____

____

____

These magical things happened today…

____

____

____

☐ I practiced **Magic Money™ maximization** today, and gave ____ %/$ to ________________ saved ____ %/$ in my opportunity chest, paid ____ %/$ for debt, put aside ____ %/$ for taxes and saved ____ %/$ for fun! It's going to be so fun to ______________________________.

Today I'm feeling ______________________________

____

The exciting things I have in store for today are ______________________________

____

Today's Magic Money™ mantra is ______________________________

____

Today's Magic Money™ intention(s): It is so amazing that…

____

____

____

I bless ______________________________

______________________________ *as good, good, good!*

Today's Magic Money™ results include:

____

____

____

These magical things happened today…

____

____

____

☐ I practiced **Magic Money™ maximization** today, and gave ____ %/$ to ________________ saved ____ %/$ in my opportunity chest, paid ____ %/$ for debt, put aside ____ %/$ for taxes and saved ____ %/$ for fun! It's going to be so fun to ______________________________.

Today I'm feeling ______________________________

____

The exciting things I have in store for today are ______________________________

____

Today's Magic Money™ mantra is ______________________________

____

Today's Magic Money™ intention(s): It is so amazing that…

____

____

____

I bless ______________________________

______________________________ *as good, good, good!*

Today's Magic Money™ results include:

____

____

____

These magical things happened today…

____

____

____

☐ I practiced **Magic Money™ maximization** today, and gave ____ %/$ to ________________ saved ____ %/$ in my opportunity chest, paid ____ %/$ for debt, put aside ____ %/$ for taxes and saved ____ %/$ for fun! It's going to be so fun to ______________________________.

Today I'm feeling ______________________________

____

The exciting things I have in store for today are ______________________________

____

Today's Magic Money™ mantra is ______________________________

____

Today's Magic Money™ intention(s): It is so amazing that…

____

____

____

I bless ______________________________

______________________________ *as good, good, good!*

Today's Magic Money™ results include:

____

____

____

These magical things happened today…

____

____

____

☐ I practiced **Magic Money™ maximization** today, and gave ____ %/$ to ________________ saved ____ %/$ in my opportunity chest, paid ____ %/$ for debt, put aside ____ %/$ for taxes and saved ____ %/$ for fun! It's going to be so fun to ______________________________.

Today I'm feeling ____________________

The exciting things I have in store for today are ____________________

Today's Magic Money™ mantra is ____________________

Today's Magic Money™ intention(s): It is so amazing that…

I bless ____________________ *as good, good, good!*

Today's Magic Money™ results include:

These magical things happened today…

☐ I practiced **Magic Money™ maximization** today, and gave ____ %/$ to ____________ saved ____ %/$ in my opportunity chest, paid ____ %/$ for debt, put aside ____ %/$ for taxes and saved ____ %/$ for fun! It's going to be so fun to ____________________.

Today I'm feeling ______________________________

____

The exciting things I have in store for today are ______________________________

____

Today's Magic Money™ mantra is ______________________________

____

Today's Magic Money™ intention(s): It is so amazing that…

____

____

____

I bless ______________________________

______________________________ *as good, good, good!*

Today's Magic Money™ results include:

____

____

____

These magical things happened today…

____

____

____

☐ I practiced **Magic Money™ maximization** today, and gave ____ %/$ to ______________ saved ____ %/$ in my opportunity chest, paid ____ %/$ for debt, put aside ____ %/$ for taxes and saved ____ %/$ for fun! It's going to be so fun to ______________________________.

Today I'm feeling ______________________________

____

The exciting things I have in store for today are ______________________________

____

Today's Magic Money™ mantra is ______________________________

____

Today's Magic Money™ intention(s): It is so amazing that…

____

____

____

I bless ______________________________

______________________________ *as good, good, good!*

Today's Magic Money™ results include:

____

____

____

These magical things happened today…

____

____

____

☐ I practiced **Magic Money™ maximization** today, and gave ____ %/$ to ________________ saved ____ %/$ in my opportunity chest, paid ____ %/$ for debt, put aside ____ %/$ for taxes and saved ____ %/$ for fun! It's going to be so fun to ______________________________.

Today I'm feeling ______________________________

____

The exciting things I have in store for today are ______________________________

____

Today's Magic Money™ mantra is ______________________________

____

Today's Magic Money™ intention(s): It is so amazing that…

____

____

____

I bless ______________________________

______________________________ *as good, good, good!*

Today's Magic Money™ results include:

____

____

____

These magical things happened today…

____

____

____

☐ I practiced **Magic Money™ maximization** today, and gave ____ %/$ to ________________ saved ____ %/$ in my opportunity chest, paid ____ %/$ for debt, put aside ____ %/$ for taxes and saved ____ %/$ for fun! It's going to be so fun to ______________________________.

Today I'm feeling ______________________________

____

The exciting things I have in store for today are ______________________________

____

Today's Magic Money™ mantra is ______________________________

____

Today's Magic Money™ intention(s): It is so amazing that…

____

____

____

I bless ______________________________

______________________________ *as good, good, good!*

Today's Magic Money™ results include:

____

____

____

These magical things happened today…

____

____

____

☐ I practiced **Magic Money™ maximization** today, and gave ____ %/$ to ______________ saved ____ %/$ in my opportunity chest, paid ____ %/$ for debt, put aside ____ %/$ for taxes and saved ____ %/$ for fun! It's going to be so fun to ______________________________.

Today I'm feeling ______________________________

____

The exciting things I have in store for today are ______________________________

____

Today's Magic Money™ mantra is ______________________________

____

Today's Magic Money™ intention(s): It is so amazing that…

____

____

____

I bless ______________________________

______________________________ *as good, good, good!*

Today's Magic Money™ results include:

____

____

____

These magical things happened today…

____

____

____

☐ I practiced **Magic Money™ maximization** today, and gave ____ %/$ to ________________ saved ____ %/$ in my opportunity chest, paid ____ %/$ for debt, put aside ____ %/$ for taxes and saved ____ %/$ for fun! It's going to be so fun to ______________________________.

Today I'm feeling ____

The exciting things I have in store for today are ____________________

Today's Magic Money™ mantra is ______________________________

Today's Magic Money™ intention(s): It is so amazing that…

I bless ____

____*as good, good, good!*

Today's Magic Money™ results include:

These magical things happened today…

☐ I practiced **Magic Money™ maximization** today, and gave ____ %/$ to ________________ saved ____ %/$ in my opportunity chest, paid ____ %/$ for debt, put aside ____ %/$ for taxes and saved ____ %/$ for fun! It's going to be so fun to __________________________________.

Today I'm feeling ______________________________

____

The exciting things I have in store for today are ______________________________

____

Today's Magic Money™ mantra is ______________________________

____

Today's Magic Money™ intention(s): It is so amazing that…

____

____

____

I bless ______________________________

______________________________ *as good, good, good!*

Today's Magic Money™ results include:

____

____

____

These magical things happened today…

____

____

____

☐ I practiced **Magic Money™ maximization** today, and gave ____ %/$ to ________________ saved ____ %/$ in my opportunity chest, paid ____ %/$ for debt, put aside ____ %/$ for taxes and saved ____ %/$ for fun! It's going to be so fun to ______________________________.

Today I'm feeling ______________________________

____

The exciting things I have in store for today are ______________________________

____

Today's Magic Money™ mantra is ______________________________

____

Today's Magic Money™ intention(s): It is so amazing that…

____

____

____

I bless ______________________________

______________________________ *as good, good, good!*

Today's Magic Money™ results include:

____

____

____

These magical things happened today…

____

____

____

☐ I practiced **Magic Money™ maximization** today, and gave ____ %/$ to ______________ saved ____ %/$ in my opportunity chest, paid ____ %/$ for debt, put aside ____ %/$ for taxes and saved ____ %/$ for fun! It's going to be so fun to ______________________________.

DATE: **$** **MAGIC MONEY DAY 60**

Today I'm feeling ______________________________

____

The exciting things I have in store for today are ______________________________

____

Today's Magic Money™ mantra is ______________________________

____

Today's Magic Money™ intention(s): It is so amazing that…

____

____

____

I bless ______________________________

______________________________*as good, good, good!*

Today's Magic Money™ results include:

____

____

____

These magical things happened today…

____

____

____

☐ I practiced **Magic Money™ maximization** today, and gave ____ %/$ to ________________ saved ____ %/$ in my opportunity chest, paid ____ %/$ for debt, put aside ____ %/$ for taxes and saved ____ %/$ for fun! It's going to be so fun to ______________________________.

YOUR FINAL MAGIC MONEY EXPERIMENT

FOR A LIFETIME OF MAGIC MONEY

Light a candle, make a cup of tea (or pour yourself a glass of something delightful), and get ready. It's time for *Magic Money Mastery.*

Here's my Magic Money™ intention:

I always have more than enough to give, save, share, and spare,
and my needs and desires are always met (on time or early).

Your Lifelong Magic Money™ Intention

In one simple sentence, write down how abundantly you want to live the rest of your life. You might want just enough to live comfortably and without stress, or you might want to become the world's 1,811th billionaire. Up to you, my friend. If you can think it, then to become it you must ink it.

Now that you've crafted your Magic Money™ intention, use the following pages to continue your daily Magic Money™ practice.

Things to Remember:

The longer you wait, the better the result.

Rejection is protection.

DATE: $ MAGIC MONEY DAY

Today I'm feeling ____

The exciting things I have in store for today are ____

Today's Magic Money™ mantra is ____

Today's Magic Money™ intention(s): It is so amazing that…

I bless ____ *as good, good, good!*

Today's Magic Money™ results include:

These magical things happened today…

DATE: $ MAGIC MONEY DAY

Today I'm feeling ____

The exciting things I have in store for today are ____

Today's Magic Money™ mantra is ____

Today's Magic Money™ intention(s): It is so amazing that…

I bless ____ *as good, good, good!*

Today's Magic Money™ results include:

These magical things happened today…

DATE: $ MAGIC MONEY DAY

Today I'm feeling ______

The exciting things I have in store for today are ______

______

Today's Magic Money™ mantra is ______

______

Today's Magic Money™ intention(s): It is so amazing that…

______

______

I bless ______ *as good, good, good!*

Today's Magic Money™ results include:

______

______

These magical things happened today…

______

DATE: $ MAGIC MONEY DAY

Today I'm feeling ______

The exciting things I have in store for today are ______

______

Today's Magic Money™ mantra is ______

______

Today's Magic Money™ intention(s): It is so amazing that…

______

______

I bless ______ *as good, good, good!*

Today's Magic Money™ results include:

______

______

These magical things happened today…

______

DATE: $ MAGIC MONEY DAY

Today I'm feeling ______________________________

The exciting things I have in store for today are ______________________________

____

Today's Magic Money™ mantra is ______________________________

____

Today's Magic Money™ intention(s): It is so amazing that…

____

____

I bless ______________________________ *as good, good, good!*

Today's Magic Money™ results include:

____

____

These magical things happened today…

____

DATE: $ MAGIC MONEY DAY

Today I'm feeling ______________________________

The exciting things I have in store for today are ______________________________

____

Today's Magic Money™ mantra is ______________________________

____

Today's Magic Money™ intention(s): It is so amazing that…

____

____

I bless ______________________________ *as good, good, good!*

Today's Magic Money™ results include:

____

____

These magical things happened today…

____

DATE: $ MAGIC MONEY DAY

Today I'm feeling ______________________________

The exciting things I have in store for today are ______________________________

____

Today's Magic Money™ mantra is ______________________________

____

Today's Magic Money™ intention(s): It is so amazing that…

____

____

I bless ______________________________ *as good, good, good!*

Today's Magic Money™ results include:

____

____

These magical things happened today…

____

I practiced **Magic Money™ maximization** this week, and gave _____ %/$ to ________________ saved _____ %/$ in my opportunity chest, paid _____ %/$ for debt, put aside _____ %/$ for taxes and saved _____ %/$ for fun! It's going to be so fun to ______________________________

______________________________.

DATE:	$	MAGIC MONEY DAY

Today I'm feeling ____________________

The exciting things I have in store for today are ____________________

____

Today's Magic Money™ mantra is ____________________

____

Today's Magic Money™ intention(s): It is so amazing that…

____

____

I bless ____________________ *as good, good, good!*

Today's Magic Money™ results include:

____

____

These magical things happened today…

____

DATE:	$	MAGIC MONEY DAY

Today I'm feeling ____________________

The exciting things I have in store for today are ____________________

____

Today's Magic Money™ mantra is ____________________

____

Today's Magic Money™ intention(s): It is so amazing that…

____

____

I bless ____________________ *as good, good, good!*

Today's Magic Money™ results include:

____

____

These magical things happened today…

____

DATE: $ MAGIC MONEY DAY

Today I'm feeling ___

The exciting things I have in store for today are ___

Today's Magic Money™ mantra is ___

Today's Magic Money™ intention(s): It is so amazing that…

I bless ___ *as good, good, good!*

Today's Magic Money™ results include:

These magical things happened today…

DATE: $ MAGIC MONEY DAY

Today I'm feeling ___

The exciting things I have in store for today are ___

Today's Magic Money™ mantra is ___

Today's Magic Money™ intention(s): It is so amazing that…

I bless ___ *as good, good, good!*

Today's Magic Money™ results include:

These magical things happened today…

DATE: $ MAGIC MONEY DAY

Today I'm feeling ___

The exciting things I have in store for today are ___

___

Today's Magic Money™ mantra is ___

___

Today's Magic Money™ intention(s): It is so amazing that…

___

___

I bless ___ *as good, good, good!*

Today's Magic Money™ results include:

___

___

These magical things happened today…

___

DATE: $ MAGIC MONEY DAY

Today I'm feeling ___

The exciting things I have in store for today are ___

___

Today's Magic Money™ mantra is ___

___

Today's Magic Money™ intention(s): It is so amazing that…

___

___

I bless ___ *as good, good, good!*

Today's Magic Money™ results include:

___

___

These magical things happened today…

___

DATE: $ MAGIC MONEY DAY

Today I'm feeling ______

The exciting things I have in store for today are ______

______

Today's Magic Money™ mantra is ______

______

Today's Magic Money™ intention(s): It is so amazing that…

______

______

I bless ______ *as good, good, good!*

Today's Magic Money™ results include:

______

______

These magical things happened today…

______

I practiced **Magic Money™ maximization** this week, and gave _____ %/$ to __________ saved _____ %/$ in my opportunity chest, paid _____ %/$ for debt, put aside _____ %/$ for taxes and saved _____ %/$ for fun! It's going to be so fun to ______________________.

DATE: $ MAGIC MONEY DAY

Today I'm feeling ______________________________

The exciting things I have in store for today are ______________________________

____

Today's Magic Money™ mantra is ______________________________

____

Today's Magic Money™ intention(s): It is so amazing that…

____

____

I bless ______________________________ *as good, good, good!*

Today's Magic Money™ results include:

____

____

These magical things happened today…

____

DATE: $ MAGIC MONEY DAY

Today I'm feeling ______________________________

The exciting things I have in store for today are ______________________________

____

Today's Magic Money™ mantra is ______________________________

____

Today's Magic Money™ intention(s): It is so amazing that…

____

____

I bless ______________________________ *as good, good, good!*

Today's Magic Money™ results include:

____

____

These magical things happened today…

____

DATE: $ MAGIC MONEY DAY

Today I'm feeling ______

The exciting things I have in store for today are ______

Today's Magic Money™ mantra is ______

Today's Magic Money™ intention(s): It is so amazing that…

I bless ______ *as good, good, good!*

Today's Magic Money™ results include:

These magical things happened today…

DATE: $ MAGIC MONEY DAY

Today I'm feeling ______

The exciting things I have in store for today are ______

Today's Magic Money™ mantra is ______

Today's Magic Money™ intention(s): It is so amazing that…

I bless ______ *as good, good, good!*

Today's Magic Money™ results include:

These magical things happened today…

DATE: $ MAGIC MONEY DAY

Today I'm feeling ______

The exciting things I have in store for today are ______

Today's Magic Money™ mantra is ______

Today's Magic Money™ intention(s): It is so amazing that…

I bless ______ *as good, good, good!*

Today's Magic Money™ results include:

These magical things happened today…

DATE: $ MAGIC MONEY DAY

Today I'm feeling ______

The exciting things I have in store for today are ______

Today's Magic Money™ mantra is ______

Today's Magic Money™ intention(s): It is so amazing that…

I bless ______ *as good, good, good!*

Today's Magic Money™ results include:

These magical things happened today…

DATE: $ MAGIC MONEY DAY

Today I'm feeling ______________________________

The exciting things I have in store for today are ______________________________

____

Today's Magic Money™ mantra is ______________________________

____

Today's Magic Money™ intention(s): It is so amazing that…

____

____

I bless ______________________________ *as good, good, good!*

Today's Magic Money™ results include:

____

____

These magical things happened today…

____

I practiced **Magic Money™ maximization** this week, and gave _____ %/$ to ________________ saved _____ %/$ in my opportunity chest, paid _____ %/$ for debt, put aside _____ %/$ for taxes and saved _____ %/$ for fun! It's going to be so fun to ______________________________

______________________________.

DATE:	$	MAGIC MONEY DAY

Today I'm feeling ______

The exciting things I have in store for today are ______

______

Today's Magic Money™ mantra is ______

______

Today's Magic Money™ intention(s): It is so amazing that…

______

______

I bless ______ *as good, good, good!*

Today's Magic Money™ results include:

______

______

These magical things happened today…

______

DATE:	$	MAGIC MONEY DAY

Today I'm feeling ______

The exciting things I have in store for today are ______

______

Today's Magic Money™ mantra is ______

______

Today's Magic Money™ intention(s): It is so amazing that…

______

______

I bless ______ *as good, good, good!*

Today's Magic Money™ results include:

______

______

These magical things happened today…

______

DATE:	$	MAGIC MONEY DAY

Today I'm feeling ______________________________

The exciting things I have in store for today are ______________________________

Today's Magic Money™ mantra is ______________________________

Today's Magic Money™ intention(s): It is so amazing that…

I bless ______________________________ *as good, good, good!*

Today's Magic Money™ results include:

These magical things happened today…

DATE:	$	MAGIC MONEY DAY

Today I'm feeling ______________________________

The exciting things I have in store for today are ______________________________

Today's Magic Money™ mantra is ______________________________

Today's Magic Money™ intention(s): It is so amazing that…

I bless ______________________________ *as good, good, good!*

Today's Magic Money™ results include:

These magical things happened today…

DATE: $ MAGIC MONEY DAY

Today I'm feeling ____________________

The exciting things I have in store for today are ____________________

____

Today's Magic Money™ mantra is ____________________

____

Today's Magic Money™ intention(s): It is so amazing that…

____

____

I bless ____________________ *as good, good, good!*

Today's Magic Money™ results include:

____

____

These magical things happened today…

____

DATE: $ MAGIC MONEY DAY

Today I'm feeling ____________________

The exciting things I have in store for today are ____________________

____

Today's Magic Money™ mantra is ____________________

____

Today's Magic Money™ intention(s): It is so amazing that…

____

____

I bless ____________________ *as good, good, good!*

Today's Magic Money™ results include:

____

____

These magical things happened today…

____

DATE: $ MAGIC MONEY DAY

Today I'm feeling ______________________________

The exciting things I have in store for today are ______________________________

____

Today's Magic Money™ mantra is ______________________________

____

Today's Magic Money™ intention(s): It is so amazing that…

____

____

I bless ______________________________ *as good, good, good!*

Today's Magic Money™ results include:

____

____

These magical things happened today…

____

I practiced **Magic Money™ maximization** this week, and gave _____ %/$ to ________________ saved _____ %/$ in my opportunity chest, paid _____ %/$ for debt, put aside _____ %/$ for taxes and saved _____ %/$ for fun! It's going to be so fun to ______________________________

______________________________.

DATE:	$	MAGIC MONEY DAY

Today I'm feeling ___

The exciting things I have in store for today are ___

___

Today's Magic Money™ mantra is ___

___

Today's Magic Money™ intention(s): It is so amazing that…

___

___

I bless ___ *as good, good, good!*

Today's Magic Money™ results include:

___

___

These magical things happened today…

___

DATE:	$	MAGIC MONEY DAY

Today I'm feeling ___

The exciting things I have in store for today are ___

___

Today's Magic Money™ mantra is ___

___

Today's Magic Money™ intention(s): It is so amazing that…

___

___

I bless ___ *as good, good, good!*

Today's Magic Money™ results include:

___

___

These magical things happened today…

___

DATE: $ MAGIC MONEY DAY

Today I'm feeling ______

The exciting things I have in store for today are ______

Today's Magic Money ™ mantra is ______

Today's Magic Money ™ intention(s): It is so amazing that…

I bless ______ *as good, good, good!*

Today's Magic Money ™ results include:

These magical things happened today…

DATE: $ MAGIC MONEY DAY

Today I'm feeling ______

The exciting things I have in store for today are ______

Today's Magic Money ™ mantra is ______

Today's Magic Money ™ intention(s): It is so amazing that…

I bless ______ *as good, good, good!*

Today's Magic Money ™ results include:

These magical things happened today…

DATE: $ MAGIC MONEY DAY

Today I'm feeling ______

The exciting things I have in store for today are ______

______

Today's Magic Money™ mantra is ______

______

Today's Magic Money™ intention(s): It is so amazing that…

______

______

I bless ______ *as good, good, good!*

Today's Magic Money™ results include:

______

______

These magical things happened today…

______

DATE: $ MAGIC MONEY DAY

Today I'm feeling ______

The exciting things I have in store for today are ______

______

Today's Magic Money™ mantra is ______

______

Today's Magic Money™ intention(s): It is so amazing that…

______

______

I bless ______ *as good, good, good!*

Today's Magic Money™ results include:

______

______

These magical things happened today…

______

DATE: $ MAGIC MONEY DAY

Today I'm feeling ____________________

The exciting things I have in store for today are ____________________

____

Today's Magic Money™ mantra is ____________________

____

Today's Magic Money™ intention(s): It is so amazing that…

____

____

I bless ____________________ *as good, good, good!*

Today's Magic Money™ results include:

____

____

These magical things happened today…

____

I practiced **Magic Money™ maximization** this week, and gave _____ %/$ to ____________________ saved _____ %/$ in my opportunity chest, paid _____ %/$ for debt, put aside _____ %/$ for taxes and saved _____ %/$ for fun! It's going to be so fun to ____________________

____________________.

DATE:	$	MAGIC MONEY DAY

Today I'm feeling ____________________

The exciting things I have in store for today are ____________________

____

Today's Magic Money™ mantra is ____________________

____

Today's Magic Money™ intention(s): It is so amazing that…

____

____

I bless ____________________ *as good, good, good!*

Today's Magic Money™ results include:

____

____

These magical things happened today…

____

DATE:	$	MAGIC MONEY DAY

Today I'm feeling ____________________

The exciting things I have in store for today are ____________________

____

Today's Magic Money™ mantra is ____________________

____

Today's Magic Money™ intention(s): It is so amazing that…

____

____

I bless ____________________ *as good, good, good!*

Today's Magic Money™ results include:

____

____

These magical things happened today…

____

DATE: $ MAGIC MONEY DAY

Today I'm feeling ______

The exciting things I have in store for today are ______

Today's Magic Money™ mantra is ______

Today's Magic Money™ intention(s): It is so amazing that…

I bless ______ *as good, good, good!*

Today's Magic Money™ results include:

These magical things happened today…

DATE: $ MAGIC MONEY DAY

Today I'm feeling ______

The exciting things I have in store for today are ______

Today's Magic Money™ mantra is ______

Today's Magic Money™ intention(s): It is so amazing that…

I bless ______ *as good, good, good!*

Today's Magic Money™ results include:

These magical things happened today…

DATE:	$	MAGIC MONEY DAY

Today I'm feeling ______

The exciting things I have in store for today are ______

______

Today's Magic Money™ mantra is ______

______

Today's Magic Money™ intention(s): It is so amazing that…

______

______

I bless ______ *as good, good, good!*

Today's Magic Money™ results include:

______

______

These magical things happened today…

______

DATE:	$	MAGIC MONEY DAY

Today I'm feeling ______

The exciting things I have in store for today are ______

______

Today's Magic Money™ mantra is ______

______

Today's Magic Money™ intention(s): It is so amazing that…

______

______

I bless ______ *as good, good, good!*

Today's Magic Money™ results include:

______

______

These magical things happened today…

______

DATE: $ MAGIC MONEY DAY

Today I'm feeling ____________________

The exciting things I have in store for today are ____________________

____

Today's Magic Money™ mantra is ____________________

____

Today's Magic Money™ intention(s): It is so amazing that…

____

____

I bless ____________________ *as good, good, good!*

Today's Magic Money™ results include:

____

____

These magical things happened today…

____

I practiced **Magic Money™ maximization** this week, and gave _____ %/$ to ________________ saved _____ %/$ in my opportunity chest, paid _____ %/$ for debt, put aside _____ %/$ for taxes and saved _____ %/$ for fun! It's going to be so fun to ____________________

____________________.

DATE:	$	MAGIC MONEY DAY

Today I'm feeling ______

The exciting things I have in store for today are ______

______

Today's Magic Money™ mantra is ______

______

Today's Magic Money™ intention(s): It is so amazing that…

______

______

I bless ______ *as good, good, good!*

Today's Magic Money™ results include:

______

______

These magical things happened today…

______

DATE:	$	MAGIC MONEY DAY

Today I'm feeling ______

The exciting things I have in store for today are ______

______

Today's Magic Money™ mantra is ______

______

Today's Magic Money™ intention(s): It is so amazing that…

______

______

I bless ______ *as good, good, good!*

Today's Magic Money™ results include:

______

______

These magical things happened today…

______

DATE: $ MAGIC MONEY DAY

Today I'm feeling ____________________

The exciting things I have in store for today are ____________________

Today's Magic Money™ mantra is ____________________

Today's Magic Money™ intention(s): It is so amazing that…

I bless ____________________ *as good, good, good!*

Today's Magic Money™ results include:

These magical things happened today…

DATE: $ MAGIC MONEY DAY

Today I'm feeling ____________________

The exciting things I have in store for today are ____________________

Today's Magic Money™ mantra is ____________________

Today's Magic Money™ intention(s): It is so amazing that…

I bless ____________________ *as good, good, good!*

Today's Magic Money™ results include:

These magical things happened today…

DATE: $ MAGIC MONEY DAY

Today I'm feeling ______

The exciting things I have in store for today are ______

______

Today's Magic Money™ mantra is ______

______

Today's Magic Money™ intention(s): It is so amazing that…

______

______

I bless ______ *as good, good, good!*

Today's Magic Money™ results include:

______

______

These magical things happened today…

______

DATE: $ MAGIC MONEY DAY

Today I'm feeling ______

The exciting things I have in store for today are ______

______

Today's Magic Money™ mantra is ______

______

Today's Magic Money™ intention(s): It is so amazing that…

______

______

I bless ______ *as good, good, good!*

Today's Magic Money™ results include:

______

______

These magical things happened today…

______

DATE: $ MAGIC MONEY DAY

Today I'm feeling ______

The exciting things I have in store for today are ______

______

Today's Magic Money™ mantra is ______

______

Today's Magic Money™ intention(s): It is so amazing that...

______

______

I bless ______ *as good, good, good!*

Today's Magic Money™ results include:

______

______

These magical things happened today...

______

I practiced **Magic Money™ maximization** this week, and gave _____ %/$ to ______ saved _____ %/$ in my opportunity chest, paid _____ %/$ for debt, put aside _____ %/$ for taxes and saved _____ %/$ for fun! It's going to be so fun to ______

______.

DATE: $ MAGIC MONEY DAY

Today I'm feeling ______________________________

The exciting things I have in store for today are ______________________________

____

Today's Magic Money™ mantra is ______________________________

____

Today's Magic Money™ intention(s): It is so amazing that…

____

____

I bless ______________________________ *as good, good, good!*

Today's Magic Money™ results include:

____

____

These magical things happened today…

____

DATE: $ MAGIC MONEY DAY

Today I'm feeling ______________________________

The exciting things I have in store for today are ______________________________

____

Today's Magic Money™ mantra is ______________________________

____

Today's Magic Money™ intention(s): It is so amazing that…

____

____

I bless ______________________________ *as good, good, good!*

Today's Magic Money™ results include:

____

____

These magical things happened today…

____

DATE: $ MAGIC MONEY DAY

Today I'm feeling ______

The exciting things I have in store for today are ______

______

Today's Magic Money™ mantra is ______

______

Today's Magic Money™ intention(s): It is so amazing that…

______

______

I bless ______ *as good, good, good!*

Today's Magic Money™ results include:

______

______

These magical things happened today…

______

DATE: $ MAGIC MONEY DAY

Today I'm feeling ______

The exciting things I have in store for today are ______

______

Today's Magic Money™ mantra is ______

______

Today's Magic Money™ intention(s): It is so amazing that…

______

______

I bless ______ *as good, good, good!*

Today's Magic Money™ results include:

______

______

These magical things happened today…

______

DATE: $ MAGIC MONEY DAY

Today I'm feeling ______________________

The exciting things I have in store for today are ______________________

____

Today's Magic Money™ mantra is ______________________

____

Today's Magic Money™ intention(s): It is so amazing that…

____

____

I bless ______________________ *as good, good, good!*

Today's Magic Money™ results include:

____

____

These magical things happened today…

____

DATE: $ MAGIC MONEY DAY

Today I'm feeling ______________________

The exciting things I have in store for today are ______________________

____

Today's Magic Money™ mantra is ______________________

____

Today's Magic Money™ intention(s): It is so amazing that…

____

____

I bless ______________________ *as good, good, good!*

Today's Magic Money™ results include:

____

____

These magical things happened today…

____

DATE: $ MAGIC MONEY DAY

Today I'm feeling ______________________

The exciting things I have in store for today are ______________________

____

Today's Magic Money™ mantra is ______________________

____

Today's Magic Money™ intention(s): It is so amazing that…

____

____

I bless ______________________ *as good, good, good!*

Today's Magic Money™ results include:

____

____

These magical things happened today…

____

I practiced **Magic Money™ maximization** this week, and gave _____ %/$ to _______________ saved _____ %/$ in my opportunity chest, paid _____ %/$ for debt, put aside _____ %/$ for taxes and saved _____ %/$ for fun! It's going to be so fun to ______________________

______________________.

DATE: $ MAGIC MONEY DAY

Today I'm feeling ____________________

The exciting things I have in store for today are ____________________

Today's Magic Money™ mantra is ____________________

Today's Magic Money™ intention(s): It is so amazing that…

I bless ____________________ *as good, good, good!*

Today's Magic Money™ results include:

These magical things happened today…

DATE: $ MAGIC MONEY DAY

Today I'm feeling ____________________

The exciting things I have in store for today are ____________________

Today's Magic Money™ mantra is ____________________

Today's Magic Money™ intention(s): It is so amazing that…

I bless ____________________ *as good, good, good!*

Today's Magic Money™ results include:

These magical things happened today…

DATE: $ MAGIC MONEY DAY

Today I'm feeling ______________________

The exciting things I have in store for today are ______________________

____

Today's Magic Money™ mantra is ______________________

____

Today's Magic Money™ intention(s): It is so amazing that…

____

____

I bless ______________________ *as good, good, good!*

Today's Magic Money™ results include:

____

____

These magical things happened today…

____

DATE: $ MAGIC MONEY DAY

Today I'm feeling ______________________

The exciting things I have in store for today are ______________________

____

Today's Magic Money™ mantra is ______________________

____

Today's Magic Money™ intention(s): It is so amazing that…

____

____

I bless ______________________ *as good, good, good!*

Today's Magic Money™ results include:

____

____

These magical things happened today…

____

DATE: $ MAGIC MONEY DAY

Today I'm feeling ______

The exciting things I have in store for today are ______

Today's Magic Money™ mantra is ______

Today's Magic Money™ intention(s): It is so amazing that…

I bless ______ *as good, good, good!*

Today's Magic Money™ results include:

These magical things happened today…

DATE: $ MAGIC MONEY DAY

Today I'm feeling ______

The exciting things I have in store for today are ______

Today's Magic Money™ mantra is ______

Today's Magic Money™ intention(s): It is so amazing that…

I bless ______ *as good, good, good!*

Today's Magic Money™ results include:

These magical things happened today…

DATE: $ MAGIC MONEY DAY

Today I'm feeling ___

The exciting things I have in store for today are ___

___

Today's Magic Money™ mantra is ___

___

Today's Magic Money™ intention(s): It is so amazing that…

___

___

I bless ___ *as good, good, good!*

Today's Magic Money™ results include:

___

___

These magical things happened today…

___

I practiced **Magic Money™ maximization** this week, and gave _____ %/$ to _________________ saved _____ %/$ in my opportunity chest, paid _____ %/$ for debt, put aside _____ %/$ for taxes and saved _____ %/$ for fun! It's going to be so fun to ___________________________________

___________________________________.

DATE:	$	MAGIC MONEY DAY

Today I'm feeling ______________________________

The exciting things I have in store for today are ______________________________

____

Today's Magic Money™ mantra is ______________________________

____

Today's Magic Money™ intention(s): It is so amazing that…

____

____

I bless ______________________________ *as good, good, good!*

Today's Magic Money™ results include:

____

____

These magical things happened today…

____

DATE:	$	MAGIC MONEY DAY

Today I'm feeling ______________________________

The exciting things I have in store for today are ______________________________

____

Today's Magic Money™ mantra is ______________________________

____

Today's Magic Money™ intention(s): It is so amazing that…

____

____

I bless ______________________________ *as good, good, good!*

Today's Magic Money™ results include:

____

____

These magical things happened today…

____

DATE: $ MAGIC MONEY DAY

Today I'm feeling ______

The exciting things I have in store for today are ______

______

Today's Magic Money™ mantra is ______

______

Today's Magic Money™ intention(s): It is so amazing that…

______

______

I bless ______ *as good, good, good!*

Today's Magic Money™ results include:

______

______

These magical things happened today…

______

DATE: $ MAGIC MONEY DAY

Today I'm feeling ______

The exciting things I have in store for today are ______

______

Today's Magic Money™ mantra is ______

______

Today's Magic Money™ intention(s): It is so amazing that…

______

______

I bless ______ *as good, good, good!*

Today's Magic Money™ results include:

______

______

These magical things happened today…

______

DATE: $ MAGIC MONEY DAY

Today I'm feeling ______________________________

The exciting things I have in store for today are ______________________________

____

Today's Magic Money™ mantra is ______________________________

____

Today's Magic Money™ intention(s): It is so amazing that…

____

____

I bless ______________________________ *as good, good, good!*

Today's Magic Money™ results include:

____

____

These magical things happened today…

____

DATE: $ MAGIC MONEY DAY

Today I'm feeling ______________________________

The exciting things I have in store for today are ______________________________

____

Today's Magic Money™ mantra is ______________________________

____

Today's Magic Money™ intention(s): It is so amazing that…

____

____

I bless ______________________________ *as good, good, good!*

Today's Magic Money™ results include:

____

____

These magical things happened today…

____

DATE: $ MAGIC MONEY DAY

Today I'm feeling ______________________________

The exciting things I have in store for today are ______________________________

____

Today's Magic Money™ mantra is ______________________________

____

Today's Magic Money™ intention(s): It is so amazing that…

____

____

I bless ______________________________ *as good, good, good!*

Today's Magic Money™ results include:

____

____

These magical things happened today…

____

I practiced **Magic Money™ maximization** this week, and gave _____ %/$ to __________________ saved _____ %/$ in my opportunity chest, paid _____ %/$ for debt, put aside _____ %/$ for taxes and saved _____ %/$ for fun! It's going to be so fun to ______________________________

______________________________.

DATE: $ MAGIC MONEY DAY

Today I'm feeling ______________________________

The exciting things I have in store for today are ______________________________

____

Today's Magic Money™ mantra is ______________________________

____

Today's Magic Money™ intention(s): It is so amazing that…

____

____

I bless ______________________________ *as good, good, good!*

Today's Magic Money™ results include:

____

____

These magical things happened today…

____

DATE: $ MAGIC MONEY DAY

Today I'm feeling ______________________________

The exciting things I have in store for today are ______________________________

____

Today's Magic Money™ mantra is ______________________________

____

Today's Magic Money™ intention(s): It is so amazing that…

____

____

I bless ______________________________ *as good, good, good!*

Today's Magic Money™ results include:

____

____

These magical things happened today…

____

DATE:	$	MAGIC MONEY DAY

Today I'm feeling ____________________

The exciting things I have in store for today are ____________________

*Today's Magic Money™ mantra is*____________________

Today's Magic Money™ intention(s): It is so amazing that…

I bless ____________________ *as good, good, good!*

Today's Magic Money™ results include:

These magical things happened today…

DATE:	$	MAGIC MONEY DAY

Today I'm feeling ____________________

The exciting things I have in store for today are ____________________

*Today's Magic Money™ mantra is*____________________

Today's Magic Money™ intention(s): It is so amazing that…

I bless ____________________ *as good, good, good!*

Today's Magic Money™ results include:

These magical things happened today…

DATE: $ MAGIC MONEY DAY

Today I'm feeling ______

The exciting things I have in store for today are ______

______

Today's Magic Money™ mantra is ______

______

Today's Magic Money™ intention(s): It is so amazing that…

______

______

I bless ______ *as good, good, good!*

Today's Magic Money™ results include:

______

______

These magical things happened today…

______

DATE: $ MAGIC MONEY DAY

Today I'm feeling ______

The exciting things I have in store for today are ______

______

Today's Magic Money™ mantra is ______

______

Today's Magic Money™ intention(s): It is so amazing that…

______

______

I bless ______ *as good, good, good!*

Today's Magic Money™ results include:

______

______

These magical things happened today…

______

DATE: $ MAGIC MONEY DAY

Today I'm feeling ______________________________

The exciting things I have in store for today are ______________________________

____

Today's Magic Money™ mantra is ______________________________

____

Today's Magic Money™ intention(s): It is so amazing that…

____

____

I bless ______________________________ *as good, good, good!*

Today's Magic Money™ results include:

____

____

These magical things happened today…

____

I practiced **Magic Money™ maximization** this week, and gave _____ %/$ to _______________ saved _____ %/$ in my opportunity chest, paid _____ %/$ for debt, put aside _____ %/$ for taxes and saved _____ %/$ for fun! It's going to be so fun to ______________________________

______________________________.

DATE: $ MAGIC MONEY DAY

Today I'm feeling __________

The exciting things I have in store for today are __________

Today's Magic Money™ mantra is __________

Today's Magic Money™ intention(s): It is so amazing that…

I bless __________ *as good, good, good!*

Today's Magic Money™ results include:

These magical things happened today…

DATE: $ MAGIC MONEY DAY

Today I'm feeling __________

The exciting things I have in store for today are __________

Today's Magic Money™ mantra is __________

Today's Magic Money™ intention(s): It is so amazing that…

I bless __________ *as good, good, good!*

Today's Magic Money™ results include:

These magical things happened today…

DATE: $ MAGIC MONEY DAY

Today I'm feeling ____________________

The exciting things I have in store for today are ____________________

Today's Magic Money™ mantra is ____________________

Today's Magic Money™ intention(s): It is so amazing that…

I bless ____________________ *as good, good, good!*

Today's Magic Money™ results include:

These magical things happened today…

DATE: $ MAGIC MONEY DAY

Today I'm feeling ____________________

The exciting things I have in store for today are ____________________

Today's Magic Money™ mantra is ____________________

Today's Magic Money™ intention(s): It is so amazing that…

I bless ____________________ *as good, good, good!*

Today's Magic Money™ results include:

These magical things happened today…

DATE:	$	MAGIC MONEY DAY

Today I'm feeling ______

The exciting things I have in store for today are ______

______

Today's Magic Money™ mantra is ______

______

Today's Magic Money™ intention(s): It is so amazing that...

______

______

I bless ______ *as good, good, good!*

Today's Magic Money™ results include:

______

______

These magical things happened today...

______

DATE:	$	MAGIC MONEY DAY

Today I'm feeling ______

The exciting things I have in store for today are ______

______

Today's Magic Money™ mantra is ______

______

Today's Magic Money™ intention(s): It is so amazing that...

______

______

I bless ______ *as good, good, good!*

Today's Magic Money™ results include:

______

______

These magical things happened today...

______

DATE: $ MAGIC MONEY DAY

Today I'm feeling ______________________________

The exciting things I have in store for today are ______________________________

____

Today's Magic Money™ mantra is ______________________________

____

Today's Magic Money™ intention(s): It is so amazing that…

____

____

I bless ______________________________ *as good, good, good!*

Today's Magic Money™ results include:

____

____

These magical things happened today…

____

I practiced **Magic Money™ maximization** this week, and gave _____ %/$ to ________________ saved _____ %/$ in my opportunity chest, paid _____ %/$ for debt, put aside _____ %/$ for taxes and saved _____ %/$ for fun! It's going to be so fun to ______________________________

______________________________.

DATE: $ MAGIC MONEY DAY

Today I'm feeling ______

The exciting things I have in store for today are ______

______

Today's Magic Money™ mantra is ______

______

Today's Magic Money™ intention(s): It is so amazing that…

______

______

I bless ______ *as good, good, good!*

Today's Magic Money™ results include:

______

______

These magical things happened today…

______

DATE: $ MAGIC MONEY DAY

Today I'm feeling ______

The exciting things I have in store for today are ______

______

Today's Magic Money™ mantra is ______

______

Today's Magic Money™ intention(s): It is so amazing that…

______

______

I bless ______ *as good, good, good!*

Today's Magic Money™ results include:

______

______

These magical things happened today…

______

DATE:	$	MAGIC MONEY DAY

Today I'm feeling __________

The exciting things I have in store for today are __________

Today's Magic Money™ mantra is __________

Today's Magic Money™ intention(s): It is so amazing that...

I bless __________ *as good, good, good!*

Today's Magic Money™ results include:

These magical things happened today...

DATE:	$	MAGIC MONEY DAY

Today I'm feeling __________

The exciting things I have in store for today are __________

Today's Magic Money™ mantra is __________

Today's Magic Money™ intention(s): It is so amazing that...

I bless __________ *as good, good, good!*

Today's Magic Money™ results include:

These magical things happened today...

DATE: $ MAGIC MONEY DAY

Today I'm feeling __________

The exciting things I have in store for today are __________

Today's Magic Money™ mantra is __________

Today's Magic Money™ intention(s): It is so amazing that…

I bless __________ *as good, good, good!*

Today's Magic Money™ results include:

These magical things happened today…

DATE: $ MAGIC MONEY DAY

Today I'm feeling __________

The exciting things I have in store for today are __________

Today's Magic Money™ mantra is __________

Today's Magic Money™ intention(s): It is so amazing that…

I bless __________ *as good, good, good!*

Today's Magic Money™ results include:

These magical things happened today…

DATE: $ MAGIC MONEY DAY

Today I'm feeling ____________________

The exciting things I have in store for today are ____________________

____

Today's Magic Money™ mantra is ____________________

____

Today's Magic Money™ intention(s): It is so amazing that…

____

____

I bless ____________________ *as good, good, good!*

Today's Magic Money™ results include:

____

____

These magical things happened today…

____

I practiced **Magic Money™ maximization** this week, and gave _____ %/$ to _________________ saved _____ %/$ in my opportunity chest, paid _____ %/$ for debt, put aside _____ %/$ for taxes and saved _____ %/$ for fun! It's going to be so fun to ____________________

____________________.

DATE: $ MAGIC MONEY DAY

Today I'm feeling ______________________________

The exciting things I have in store for today are ______________________________

____

Today's Magic Money™ mantra is ______________________________

____

Today's Magic Money™ intention(s): It is so amazing that…

____

____

I bless ______________________________ *as good, good, good!*

Today's Magic Money™ results include:

____

____

These magical things happened today…

____

DATE: $ MAGIC MONEY DAY

Today I'm feeling ______________________________

The exciting things I have in store for today are ______________________________

____

Today's Magic Money™ mantra is ______________________________

____

Today's Magic Money™ intention(s): It is so amazing that…

____

____

I bless ______________________________ *as good, good, good!*

Today's Magic Money™ results include:

____

____

These magical things happened today…

____

DATE: $ MAGIC MONEY DAY

Today I'm feeling ______

The exciting things I have in store for today are ______

Today's Magic Money™ mantra is ______

Today's Magic Money™ intention(s): It is so amazing that…

I bless ______ *as good, good, good!*

Today's Magic Money™ results include:

These magical things happened today…

DATE: $ MAGIC MONEY DAY

Today I'm feeling ______

The exciting things I have in store for today are ______

Today's Magic Money™ mantra is ______

Today's Magic Money™ intention(s): It is so amazing that…

I bless ______ *as good, good, good!*

Today's Magic Money™ results include:

These magical things happened today…

DATE:	$	MAGIC MONEY DAY

Today I'm feeling ______

The exciting things I have in store for today are ______

Today's Magic Money™ mantra is ______

Today's Magic Money™ intention(s): It is so amazing that…

I bless ______ *as good, good, good!*

Today's Magic Money™ results include:

These magical things happened today…

DATE:	$	MAGIC MONEY DAY

Today I'm feeling ______

The exciting things I have in store for today are ______

Today's Magic Money™ mantra is ______

Today's Magic Money™ intention(s): It is so amazing that…

I bless ______ *as good, good, good!*

Today's Magic Money™ results include:

These magical things happened today…

DATE: $ MAGIC MONEY DAY

Today I'm feeling ______________________________

The exciting things I have in store for today are ______________________________

____

Today's Magic Money™ mantra is ______________________________

____

Today's Magic Money™ intention(s): It is so amazing that…

____

____

I bless ______________________________ *as good, good, good!*

Today's Magic Money™ results include:

____

____

These magical things happened today…

____

I practiced **Magic Money™ maximization** this week, and gave _____ %/$ to __________________ saved _____ %/$ in my opportunity chest, paid _____ %/$ for debt, put aside _____ %/$ for taxes and saved _____ %/$ for fun! It's going to be so fun to ______________________________

______________________________.

DATE: $ MAGIC MONEY DAY

Today I'm feeling ______________________________

The exciting things I have in store for today are ______________________________

____

Today's Magic Money™ mantra is ______________________________

____

Today's Magic Money™ intention(s): It is so amazing that…

____

____

I bless ______________________________ *as good, good, good!*

Today's Magic Money™ results include:

____

____

These magical things happened today…

____

DATE: $ MAGIC MONEY DAY

Today I'm feeling ______________________________

The exciting things I have in store for today are ______________________________

____

Today's Magic Money™ mantra is ______________________________

____

Today's Magic Money™ intention(s): It is so amazing that…

____

____

I bless ______________________________ *as good, good, good!*

Today's Magic Money™ results include:

____

____

These magical things happened today…

____

DATE: $ MAGIC MONEY DAY

Today I'm feeling ______

The exciting things I have in store for today are ______

Today's Magic Money™ mantra is ______

Today's Magic Money™ intention(s): It is so amazing that…

I bless ______ *as good, good, good!*

Today's Magic Money™ results include:

These magical things happened today…

DATE: $ MAGIC MONEY DAY

Today I'm feeling ______

The exciting things I have in store for today are ______

Today's Magic Money™ mantra is ______

Today's Magic Money™ intention(s): It is so amazing that…

I bless ______ *as good, good, good!*

Today's Magic Money™ results include:

These magical things happened today…

DATE: $ MAGIC MONEY DAY

Today I'm feeling ______________________

The exciting things I have in store for today are ______________________

____

Today's Magic Money™ mantra is ______________________

____

Today's Magic Money™ intention(s): It is so amazing that…

____

____

I bless ______________________ *as good, good, good!*

Today's Magic Money™ results include:

____

____

These magical things happened today…

____

DATE: $ MAGIC MONEY DAY

Today I'm feeling ______________________

The exciting things I have in store for today are ______________________

____

Today's Magic Money™ mantra is ______________________

____

Today's Magic Money™ intention(s): It is so amazing that…

____

____

I bless ______________________ *as good, good, good!*

Today's Magic Money™ results include:

____

____

These magical things happened today…

____

DATE: $ MAGIC MONEY DAY

Today I'm feeling ______________________

The exciting things I have in store for today are ______________________

____

Today's Magic Money™ mantra is ______________________

____

Today's Magic Money™ intention(s): It is so amazing that…

____

____

I bless ______________________ *as good, good, good!*

Today's Magic Money™ results include:

____

____

These magical things happened today…

____

I practiced **Magic Money™ maximization** this week, and gave _____ %/$ to ______________ saved _____ %/$ in my opportunity chest, paid _____ %/$ for debt, put aside _____ %/$ for taxes and saved _____ %/$ for fun! It's going to be so fun to ______________________

______________________.

DATE: $ MAGIC MONEY DAY

Today I'm feeling ______

The exciting things I have in store for today are ______

______

Today's Magic Money™ mantra is ______

______

Today's Magic Money™ intention(s): It is so amazing that…

______

______

I bless ______ *as good, good, good!*

Today's Magic Money™ results include:

______

______

These magical things happened today…

______

DATE: $ MAGIC MONEY DAY

Today I'm feeling ______

The exciting things I have in store for today are ______

______

Today's Magic Money™ mantra is ______

______

Today's Magic Money™ intention(s): It is so amazing that…

______

______

I bless ______ *as good, good, good!*

Today's Magic Money™ results include:

______

______

These magical things happened today…

______

DATE: $ MAGIC MONEY DAY

Today I'm feeling ______________________________

The exciting things I have in store for today are ______________________________

____

Today's Magic Money™ mantra is ______________________________

____

Today's Magic Money™ intention(s): It is so amazing that…

____

____

I bless ______________________________ *as good, good, good!*

Today's Magic Money™ results include:

____

____

These magical things happened today…

____

DATE: $ MAGIC MONEY DAY

Today I'm feeling ______________________________

The exciting things I have in store for today are ______________________________

____

Today's Magic Money™ mantra is ______________________________

____

Today's Magic Money™ intention(s): It is so amazing that…

____

____

I bless ______________________________ *as good, good, good!*

Today's Magic Money™ results include:

____

____

These magical things happened today…

____

DATE: $ MAGIC MONEY DAY

Today I'm feeling __________

The exciting things I have in store for today are __________

Today's Magic Money™ mantra is __________

Today's Magic Money™ intention(s): It is so amazing that…

I bless __________ *as good, good, good!*

Today's Magic Money™ results include:

These magical things happened today…

DATE: $ MAGIC MONEY DAY

Today I'm feeling __________

The exciting things I have in store for today are __________

Today's Magic Money™ mantra is __________

Today's Magic Money™ intention(s): It is so amazing that…

I bless __________ *as good, good, good!*

Today's Magic Money™ results include:

These magical things happened today…

DATE: $ MAGIC MONEY DAY

Today I'm feeling ______________________________

The exciting things I have in store for today are ______________________________

____

Today's Magic Money™ mantra is ______________________________

____

Today's Magic Money™ intention(s): It is so amazing that…

____

____

I bless ______________________________ *as good, good, good!*

Today's Magic Money™ results include:

____

____

These magical things happened today…

____

I practiced **Magic Money™ maximization** this week, and gave _____ %/$ to __________ saved _____ %/$ in my opportunity chest, paid _____ %/$ for debt, put aside _____ %/$ for taxes and saved _____ %/$ for fun! It's going to be so fun to ______________________________

______________________________.

DATE: $ MAGIC MONEY DAY

Today I'm feeling ____________________

The exciting things I have in store for today are ____________________

Today's Magic Money™ mantra is ____________________

Today's Magic Money™ intention(s): It is so amazing that…

I bless ____________________ *as good, good, good!*

Today's Magic Money™ results include:

These magical things happened today…

DATE: $ MAGIC MONEY DAY

Today I'm feeling ____________________

The exciting things I have in store for today are ____________________

Today's Magic Money™ mantra is ____________________

Today's Magic Money™ intention(s): It is so amazing that…

I bless ____________________ *as good, good, good!*

Today's Magic Money™ results include:

These magical things happened today…

DATE: $ MAGIC MONEY DAY

Today I'm feeling ____________________

The exciting things I have in store for today are ____________________

Today's Magic Money™ mantra is ____________________

Today's Magic Money™ intention(s): It is so amazing that…

I bless ____________________ *as good, good, good!*

Today's Magic Money™ results include:

These magical things happened today…

DATE: $ MAGIC MONEY DAY

Today I'm feeling ____________________

The exciting things I have in store for today are ____________________

Today's Magic Money™ mantra is ____________________

Today's Magic Money™ intention(s): It is so amazing that…

I bless ____________________ *as good, good, good!*

Today's Magic Money™ results include:

These magical things happened today…

DATE: $ MAGIC MONEY DAY

Today I'm feeling ______________________________

The exciting things I have in store for today are ______________________________

____

Today's Magic Money™ mantra is ______________________________

____

Today's Magic Money™ intention(s): It is so amazing that…

____

____

I bless ______________________________ *as good, good, good!*

Today's Magic Money™ results include:

____

____

These magical things happened today…

____

DATE: $ MAGIC MONEY DAY

Today I'm feeling ______________________________

The exciting things I have in store for today are ______________________________

____

Today's Magic Money™ mantra is ______________________________

____

Today's Magic Money™ intention(s): It is so amazing that…

____

____

I bless ______________________________ *as good, good, good!*

Today's Magic Money™ results include:

____

____

These magical things happened today…

____

DATE: $ MAGIC MONEY DAY

Today I'm feeling ______________________________

The exciting things I have in store for today are ______________________________

____

Today's Magic Money™ mantra is ______________________________

____

Today's Magic Money™ intention(s): It is so amazing that…

____

____

I bless ______________________________ *as good, good, good!*

Today's Magic Money™ results include:

____

____

These magical things happened today…

____

I practiced **Magic Money™ maximization** this week, and gave _____ %/$ to __________________ saved _____ %/$ in my opportunity chest, paid _____ %/$ for debt, put aside _____ %/$ for taxes and saved _____ %/$ for fun! It's going to be so fun to ______________________________

______________________________.

DATE: $ MAGIC MONEY DAY

Today I'm feeling __________

The exciting things I have in store for today are __________

Today's Magic Money™ mantra is __________

Today's Magic Money™ intention(s): It is so amazing that…

I bless __________ *as good, good, good!*

Today's Magic Money™ results include:

These magical things happened today…

DATE: $ MAGIC MONEY DAY

Today I'm feeling __________

The exciting things I have in store for today are __________

Today's Magic Money™ mantra is __________

Today's Magic Money™ intention(s): It is so amazing that…

I bless __________ *as good, good, good!*

Today's Magic Money™ results include:

These magical things happened today…

DATE: $ MAGIC MONEY DAY

Today I'm feeling ______________________

The exciting things I have in store for today are ______________________

____

Today's Magic Money™ mantra is ______________________

____

Today's Magic Money™ intention(s): It is so amazing that…

____

____

I bless ______________________ *as good, good, good!*

Today's Magic Money™ results include:

____

____

These magical things happened today…

____

DATE: $ MAGIC MONEY DAY

Today I'm feeling ______________________

The exciting things I have in store for today are ______________________

____

Today's Magic Money™ mantra is ______________________

____

Today's Magic Money™ intention(s): It is so amazing that…

____

____

I bless ______________________ *as good, good, good!*

Today's Magic Money™ results include:

____

____

These magical things happened today…

____

DATE:	$	MAGIC MONEY DAY

Today I'm feeling ______

The exciting things I have in store for today are ______

______

Today's Magic Money™ mantra is ______

______

Today's Magic Money™ intention(s): It is so amazing that…

______

______

I bless ______ *as good, good, good!*

Today's Magic Money™ results include:

______

______

These magical things happened today…

______

DATE:	$	MAGIC MONEY DAY

Today I'm feeling ______

The exciting things I have in store for today are ______

______

Today's Magic Money™ mantra is ______

______

Today's Magic Money™ intention(s): It is so amazing that…

______

______

I bless ______ *as good, good, good!*

Today's Magic Money™ results include:

______

______

These magical things happened today…

______

DATE: $ MAGIC MONEY DAY

Today I'm feeling ______________________________

The exciting things I have in store for today are ______________________________

____

Today's Magic Money™ mantra is ______________________________

____

Today's Magic Money™ intention(s): It is so amazing that…

____

____

I bless ______________________________ *as good, good, good!*

Today's Magic Money™ results include:

____

____

These magical things happened today…

____

I practiced **Magic Money™ maximization** this week, and gave _____ %/$ to ________________ saved _____ %/$ in my opportunity chest, paid _____ %/$ for debt, put aside _____ %/$ for taxes and saved _____ %/$ for fun! It's going to be so fun to ______________________________

______________________________.

DATE: $ MAGIC MONEY DAY

Today I'm feeling __________

The exciting things I have in store for today are __________

Today's Magic Money™ mantra is __________

Today's Magic Money™ intention(s): It is so amazing that…

I bless __________ *as good, good, good!*

Today's Magic Money™ results include:

These magical things happened today…

DATE: $ MAGIC MONEY DAY

Today I'm feeling __________

The exciting things I have in store for today are __________

Today's Magic Money™ mantra is __________

Today's Magic Money™ intention(s): It is so amazing that…

I bless __________ *as good, good, good!*

Today's Magic Money™ results include:

These magical things happened today…

DATE: $ MAGIC MONEY DAY

Today I'm feeling __________

The exciting things I have in store for today are __________

Today's Magic Money™ mantra is __________

Today's Magic Money™ intention(s): It is so amazing that…

I bless __________ *as good, good, good!*

Today's Magic Money™ results include:

These magical things happened today…

DATE: $ MAGIC MONEY DAY

Today I'm feeling __________

The exciting things I have in store for today are __________

Today's Magic Money™ mantra is __________

Today's Magic Money™ intention(s): It is so amazing that…

I bless __________ *as good, good, good!*

Today's Magic Money™ results include:

These magical things happened today…

DATE:	$	MAGIC MONEY DAY

Today I'm feeling ______

The exciting things I have in store for today are ______

______

Today's Magic Money™ mantra is ______

______

Today's Magic Money™ intention(s): It is so amazing that…

______

______

I bless ______ *as good, good, good!*

Today's Magic Money™ results include:

______

______

These magical things happened today…

______

DATE:	$	MAGIC MONEY DAY

Today I'm feeling ______

The exciting things I have in store for today are ______

______

Today's Magic Money™ mantra is ______

______

Today's Magic Money™ intention(s): It is so amazing that…

______

______

I bless ______ *as good, good, good!*

Today's Magic Money™ results include:

______

______

These magical things happened today…

______

DATE: $ MAGIC MONEY DAY

Today I'm feeling ______________________

The exciting things I have in store for today are ______________________

____

Today's Magic Money™ mantra is ______________________

____

Today's Magic Money™ intention(s): It is so amazing that…

____

____

I bless ______________________ *as good, good, good!*

Today's Magic Money™ results include:

____

____

These magical things happened today…

____

I practiced **Magic Money™ maximization** this week, and gave _____ %/$ to _________________ saved _____ %/$ in my opportunity chest, paid _____ %/$ for debt, put aside _____ %/$ for taxes and saved _____ %/$ for fun! It's going to be so fun to ______________________

______________________.

DATE: $ MAGIC MONEY DAY

Today I'm feeling ______

The exciting things I have in store for today are ______

Today's Magic Money™ mantra is ______

Today's Magic Money™ intention(s): It is so amazing that…

I bless ______ *as good, good, good!*

Today's Magic Money™ results include:

These magical things happened today…

DATE: $ MAGIC MONEY DAY

Today I'm feeling ______

The exciting things I have in store for today are ______

Today's Magic Money™ mantra is ______

Today's Magic Money™ intention(s): It is so amazing that…

I bless ______ *as good, good, good!*

Today's Magic Money™ results include:

These magical things happened today…

DATE: $ MAGIC MONEY DAY

Today I'm feeling ____________________

The exciting things I have in store for today are ____________________

Today's Magic Money™ mantra is ____________________

Today's Magic Money™ intention(s): It is so amazing that…

I bless ____________________ *as good, good, good!*

Today's Magic Money™ results include:

These magical things happened today…

DATE: $ MAGIC MONEY DAY

Today I'm feeling ____________________

The exciting things I have in store for today are ____________________

Today's Magic Money™ mantra is ____________________

Today's Magic Money™ intention(s): It is so amazing that…

I bless ____________________ *as good, good, good!*

Today's Magic Money™ results include:

These magical things happened today…

DATE: $ MAGIC MONEY DAY

Today I'm feeling ____________________

The exciting things I have in store for today are ____________________

Today's Magic Money™ mantra is ____________________

Today's Magic Money™ intention(s): It is so amazing that…

I bless ____________________ *as good, good, good!*

Today's Magic Money™ results include:

These magical things happened today…

DATE: $ MAGIC MONEY DAY

Today I'm feeling ____________________

The exciting things I have in store for today are ____________________

Today's Magic Money™ mantra is ____________________

Today's Magic Money™ intention(s): It is so amazing that…

I bless ____________________ *as good, good, good!*

Today's Magic Money™ results include:

These magical things happened today…

DATE: $ MAGIC MONEY DAY

Today I'm feeling ______

The exciting things I have in store for today are ______

______

Today's Magic Money™ mantra is ______

______

Today's Magic Money™ intention(s): It is so amazing that…

______

______

I bless ______ *as good, good, good!*

Today's Magic Money™ results include:

______

______

These magical things happened today…

______

I practiced **Magic Money™ maximization** this week, and gave _____ %/$ to __________ saved _____ %/$ in my opportunity chest, paid _____ %/$ for debt, put aside _____ %/$ for taxes and saved _____ %/$ for fun! It's going to be so fun to ______

______.

DATE:	$	MAGIC MONEY DAY

Today I'm feeling ______

The exciting things I have in store for today are ______

______

Today's Magic Money™ mantra is ______

______

Today's Magic Money™ intention(s): It is so amazing that…

______

______

I bless ______ *as good, good, good!*

Today's Magic Money™ results include:

______

______

These magical things happened today…

______

DATE:	$	MAGIC MONEY DAY

Today I'm feeling ______

The exciting things I have in store for today are ______

______

Today's Magic Money™ mantra is ______

______

Today's Magic Money™ intention(s): It is so amazing that…

______

______

I bless ______ *as good, good, good!*

Today's Magic Money™ results include:

______

______

These magical things happened today…

______

DATE: $ MAGIC MONEY DAY

Today I'm feeling ______

The exciting things I have in store for today are ______

______

Today's Magic Money™ mantra is ______

______

Today's Magic Money™ intention(s): It is so amazing that…

______

______

I bless ______ *as good, good, good!*

Today's Magic Money™ results include:

______

______

These magical things happened today…

______

DATE: $ MAGIC MONEY DAY

Today I'm feeling ______

The exciting things I have in store for today are ______

______

Today's Magic Money™ mantra is ______

______

Today's Magic Money™ intention(s): It is so amazing that…

______

______

I bless ______ *as good, good, good!*

Today's Magic Money™ results include:

______

______

These magical things happened today…

______

DATE: $ MAGIC MONEY DAY

Today I'm feeling ______________________________

The exciting things I have in store for today are ______________________________

____

Today's Magic Money™ mantra is ______________________________

____

Today's Magic Money™ intention(s): It is so amazing that…

____

____

I bless ______________________________ *as good, good, good!*

Today's Magic Money™ results include:

____

____

These magical things happened today…

____

DATE: $ MAGIC MONEY DAY

Today I'm feeling ______________________________

The exciting things I have in store for today are ______________________________

____

Today's Magic Money™ mantra is ______________________________

____

Today's Magic Money™ intention(s): It is so amazing that…

____

____

I bless ______________________________ *as good, good, good!*

Today's Magic Money™ results include:

____

____

These magical things happened today…

____

DATE: $ MAGIC MONEY DAY

Today I'm feeling ______________________

The exciting things I have in store for today are ______________________

____

Today's Magic Money™ mantra is ______________________

____

Today's Magic Money™ intention(s): It is so amazing that…

____

____

I bless ______________________ *as good, good, good!*

Today's Magic Money™ results include:

____

____

These magical things happened today…

____

I practiced **Magic Money™ maximization** this week, and gave _____ %/$ to __________________ saved _____ %/$ in my opportunity chest, paid _____ %/$ for debt, put aside _____ %/$ for taxes and saved _____ %/$ for fun! It's going to be so fun to ______________________

______________________.

DATE: $ MAGIC MONEY DAY

Today I'm feeling ______

The exciting things I have in store for today are ______

______

Today's Magic Money™ mantra is ______

______

Today's Magic Money™ intention(s): It is so amazing that…

______

______

I bless ______ *as good, good, good!*

Today's Magic Money™ results include:

______

______

These magical things happened today…

______

DATE: $ MAGIC MONEY DAY

Today I'm feeling ______

The exciting things I have in store for today are ______

______

Today's Magic Money™ mantra is ______

______

Today's Magic Money™ intention(s): It is so amazing that…

______

______

I bless ______ *as good, good, good!*

Today's Magic Money™ results include:

______

______

These magical things happened today…

______

DATE: $ MAGIC MONEY DAY

Today I'm feeling ____________________

The exciting things I have in store for today are ____________________

Today's Magic Money™ mantra is ____________________

Today's Magic Money™ intention(s): It is so amazing that…

I bless ____________________ *as good, good, good!*

Today's Magic Money™ results include:

These magical things happened today…

DATE: $ MAGIC MONEY DAY

Today I'm feeling ____________________

The exciting things I have in store for today are ____________________

Today's Magic Money™ mantra is ____________________

Today's Magic Money™ intention(s): It is so amazing that…

I bless ____________________ *as good, good, good!*

Today's Magic Money™ results include:

These magical things happened today…

DATE: $ MAGIC MONEY DAY

Today I'm feeling ______

The exciting things I have in store for today are ______

Today's Magic Money™ mantra is ______

Today's Magic Money™ intention(s): It is so amazing that…

I bless ______ *as good, good, good!*

Today's Magic Money™ results include:

These magical things happened today…

DATE: $ MAGIC MONEY DAY

Today I'm feeling ______

The exciting things I have in store for today are ______

Today's Magic Money™ mantra is ______

Today's Magic Money™ intention(s): It is so amazing that…

I bless ______ *as good, good, good!*

Today's Magic Money™ results include:

These magical things happened today…

DATE: $ MAGIC MONEY DAY

Today I'm feeling ______________________________

The exciting things I have in store for today are ______________________________

____

Today's Magic Money™ mantra is ______________________________

____

Today's Magic Money™ intention(s): It is so amazing that…

____

____

I bless ______________________________ *as good, good, good!*

Today's Magic Money™ results include:

____

____

These magical things happened today…

____

I practiced **Magic Money™ maximization** this week, and gave _____ %/$ to ________________ saved _____ %/$ in my opportunity chest, paid _____ %/$ for debt, put aside _____ %/$ for taxes and saved _____ %/$ for fun! It's going to be so fun to ______________________________

______________________________.

DATE: $ MAGIC MONEY DAY

Today I'm feeling ___

The exciting things I have in store for today are ___

Today's Magic Money™ mantra is ___

Today's Magic Money™ intention(s): It is so amazing that…

I bless ___ *as good, good, good!*

Today's Magic Money™ results include:

These magical things happened today…

DATE: $ MAGIC MONEY DAY

Today I'm feeling ___

The exciting things I have in store for today are ___

Today's Magic Money™ mantra is ___

Today's Magic Money™ intention(s): It is so amazing that…

I bless ___ *as good, good, good!*

Today's Magic Money™ results include:

These magical things happened today…

DATE: $ MAGIC MONEY DAY

Today I'm feeling ______

The exciting things I have in store for today are ______

Today's Magic Money™ mantra is ______

Today's Magic Money™ intention(s): It is so amazing that…

I bless ______ *as good, good, good!*

Today's Magic Money™ results include:

These magical things happened today…

DATE: $ MAGIC MONEY DAY

Today I'm feeling ______

The exciting things I have in store for today are ______

Today's Magic Money™ mantra is ______

Today's Magic Money™ intention(s): It is so amazing that…

I bless ______ *as good, good, good!*

Today's Magic Money™ results include:

These magical things happened today…

DATE: $ MAGIC MONEY DAY

Today I'm feeling ______________________

The exciting things I have in store for today are ______________________

____

Today's Magic Money™ mantra is ______________________

____

Today's Magic Money™ intention(s): It is so amazing that…

____

____

I bless ______________________ *as good, good, good!*

Today's Magic Money™ results include:

____

____

These magical things happened today…

____

DATE: $ MAGIC MONEY DAY

Today I'm feeling ______________________

The exciting things I have in store for today are ______________________

____

Today's Magic Money™ mantra is ______________________

____

Today's Magic Money™ intention(s): It is so amazing that…

____

____

I bless ______________________ *as good, good, good!*

Today's Magic Money™ results include:

____

____

These magical things happened today…

____

DATE:	$	MAGIC MONEY DAY

Today I'm feeling ______________________________

The exciting things I have in store for today are ______________________________

____

Today's Magic Money™ mantra is ______________________________

____

Today's Magic Money™ intention(s): It is so amazing that…

____

____

I bless ______________________________ *as good, good, good!*

Today's Magic Money™ results include:

____

____

These magical things happened today…

____

I practiced **Magic Money™ maximization** this week, and gave _____ %/$ to ________________ saved _____ %/$ in my opportunity chest, paid _____ %/$ for debt, put aside _____ %/$ for taxes and saved _____ %/$ for fun! It's going to be so fun to ______________________________

______________________________.

DATE: $ MAGIC MONEY DAY

Today I'm feeling ____________________

The exciting things I have in store for today are ____________________

____

Today's Magic Money™ mantra is ____________________

____

Today's Magic Money™ intention(s): It is so amazing that…

____

____

I bless ____________________ *as good, good, good!*

Today's Magic Money™ results include:

____

____

These magical things happened today…

____

DATE: $ MAGIC MONEY DAY

Today I'm feeling ____________________

The exciting things I have in store for today are ____________________

____

Today's Magic Money™ mantra is ____________________

____

Today's Magic Money™ intention(s): It is so amazing that…

____

____

I bless ____________________ *as good, good, good!*

Today's Magic Money™ results include:

____

____

These magical things happened today…

____

DATE: $ MAGIC MONEY DAY

Today I'm feeling ______________________________

The exciting things I have in store for today are ______________________________

____

Today's Magic Money™ mantra is ______________________________

____

Today's Magic Money™ intention(s): It is so amazing that…

____

____

I bless ______________________________ *as good, good, good!*

Today's Magic Money™ results include:

____

____

These magical things happened today…

____

DATE: $ MAGIC MONEY DAY

Today I'm feeling ______________________________

The exciting things I have in store for today are ______________________________

____

Today's Magic Money™ mantra is ______________________________

____

Today's Magic Money™ intention(s): It is so amazing that…

____

____

I bless ______________________________ *as good, good, good!*

Today's Magic Money™ results include:

____

____

These magical things happened today…

____

DATE: $ MAGIC MONEY DAY

Today I'm feeling ____________________

The exciting things I have in store for today are ____________________

Today's Magic Money™ mantra is ____________________

Today's Magic Money™ intention(s): It is so amazing that…

I bless ____________________ *as good, good, good!*

Today's Magic Money™ results include:

These magical things happened today…

DATE: $ MAGIC MONEY DAY

Today I'm feeling ____________________

The exciting things I have in store for today are ____________________

Today's Magic Money™ mantra is ____________________

Today's Magic Money™ intention(s): It is so amazing that…

I bless ____________________ *as good, good, good!*

Today's Magic Money™ results include:

These magical things happened today…

DATE: $ MAGIC MONEY DAY

Today I'm feeling ____

The exciting things I have in store for today are ____________________________

____

*Today's Magic Money™ mantra is*_____________________________________

____

Today's Magic Money™ intention(s): It is so amazing that…

____

____

I bless ____*as good, good, good!*

Today's Magic Money™ results include:

____

____

These magical things happened today…

____

I practiced **Magic Money™ maximization** this week, and gave _____ %/$ to __________________ saved _____ %/$ in my opportunity chest, paid _____ %/$ for debt, put aside _____ %/$ for taxes and saved _____ %/$ for fun! It's going to be so fun to ____.

DATE: $ MAGIC MONEY DAY

Today I'm feeling ______

The exciting things I have in store for today are ______

______

Today's Magic Money™ mantra is ______

______

Today's Magic Money™ intention(s): It is so amazing that…

______

______

I bless ______ *as good, good, good!*

Today's Magic Money™ results include:

______

______

These magical things happened today…

______

DATE: $ MAGIC MONEY DAY

Today I'm feeling ______

The exciting things I have in store for today are ______

______

Today's Magic Money™ mantra is ______

______

Today's Magic Money™ intention(s): It is so amazing that…

______

______

I bless ______ *as good, good, good!*

Today's Magic Money™ results include:

______

______

These magical things happened today…

______

DATE: $ MAGIC MONEY DAY

Today I'm feeling ____________________

The exciting things I have in store for today are ____________________

Today's Magic Money™ mantra is ____________________

Today's Magic Money™ intention(s): It is so amazing that…

I bless ____________________ *as good, good, good!*

Today's Magic Money™ results include:

These magical things happened today…

DATE: $ MAGIC MONEY DAY

Today I'm feeling ____________________

The exciting things I have in store for today are ____________________

Today's Magic Money™ mantra is ____________________

Today's Magic Money™ intention(s): It is so amazing that…

I bless ____________________ *as good, good, good!*

Today's Magic Money™ results include:

These magical things happened today…

DATE: $ MAGIC MONEY DAY

Today I'm feeling ______

The exciting things I have in store for today are ______

______

Today's Magic Money™ mantra is ______

______

Today's Magic Money™ intention(s): It is so amazing that…

______

______

I bless ______ *as good, good, good!*

Today's Magic Money™ results include:

______

______

These magical things happened today…

______

DATE: $ MAGIC MONEY DAY

Today I'm feeling ______

The exciting things I have in store for today are ______

______

Today's Magic Money™ mantra is ______

______

Today's Magic Money™ intention(s): It is so amazing that…

______

______

I bless ______ *as good, good, good!*

Today's Magic Money™ results include:

______

______

These magical things happened today…

______

DATE: $ MAGIC MONEY DAY

Today I'm feeling ______________________________

The exciting things I have in store for today are ______________________________

____

Today's Magic Money™ mantra is ______________________________

____

Today's Magic Money™ intention(s): It is so amazing that…

____

____

I bless ______________________________ *as good, good, good!*

Today's Magic Money™ results include:

____

____

These magical things happened today…

____

I practiced **Magic Money™ maximization** this week, and gave _____ %/$ to _________________ saved _____ %/$ in my opportunity chest, paid _____ %/$ for debt, put aside _____ %/$ for taxes and saved _____ %/$ for fun! It's going to be so fun to ______________________________

______________________________.

DATE: $ MAGIC MONEY DAY

Today I'm feeling ________________

The exciting things I have in store for today are ________________

____

Today's Magic Money™ mantra is ________________

____

Today's Magic Money™ intention(s): It is so amazing that…

____

____

I bless ________________ *as good, good, good!*

Today's Magic Money™ results include:

____

____

These magical things happened today…

____

DATE: $ MAGIC MONEY DAY

Today I'm feeling ________________

The exciting things I have in store for today are ________________

____

Today's Magic Money™ mantra is ________________

____

Today's Magic Money™ intention(s): It is so amazing that…

____

____

I bless ________________ *as good, good, good!*

Today's Magic Money™ results include:

____

____

These magical things happened today…

____

DATE: $ MAGIC MONEY DAY

Today I'm feeling ______

The exciting things I have in store for today are ______

Today's Magic Money™ mantra is ______

Today's Magic Money™ intention(s): It is so amazing that…

I bless ______ *as good, good, good!*

Today's Magic Money™ results include:

These magical things happened today…

DATE: $ MAGIC MONEY DAY

Today I'm feeling ______

The exciting things I have in store for today are ______

Today's Magic Money™ mantra is ______

Today's Magic Money™ intention(s): It is so amazing that…

I bless ______ *as good, good, good!*

Today's Magic Money™ results include:

These magical things happened today…

DATE: $ MAGIC MONEY DAY

Today I'm feeling ______

The exciting things I have in store for today are ______

______

Today's Magic Money™ mantra is ______

______

Today's Magic Money™ intention(s): It is so amazing that…

______

______

I bless ______ *as good, good, good!*

Today's Magic Money™ results include:

______

______

These magical things happened today…

______

DATE: $ MAGIC MONEY DAY

Today I'm feeling ______

The exciting things I have in store for today are ______

______

Today's Magic Money™ mantra is ______

______

Today's Magic Money™ intention(s): It is so amazing that…

______

______

I bless ______ *as good, good, good!*

Today's Magic Money™ results include:

______

______

These magical things happened today…

______

DATE:	$	MAGIC MONEY DAY

Today I'm feeling ______________________________

The exciting things I have in store for today are ______________________________

____

Today's Magic Money™ mantra is ______________________________

____

Today's Magic Money™ intention(s): It is so amazing that…

____

____

I bless ______________________________ *as good, good, good!*

Today's Magic Money™ results include:

____

____

These magical things happened today…

____

I practiced **Magic Money™ maximization** this week, and gave _____ %/$ to __________________ saved _____ %/$ in my opportunity chest, paid _____ %/$ for debt, put aside _____ %/$ for taxes and saved _____ %/$ for fun! It's going to be so fun to ______________________________ ______________________________.

DATE: $ MAGIC MONEY DAY

Today I'm feeling ______

The exciting things I have in store for today are ______

______

Today's Magic Money™ mantra is ______

______

Today's Magic Money™ intention(s): It is so amazing that…

______

______

I bless ______ *as good, good, good!*

Today's Magic Money™ results include:

______

______

These magical things happened today…

______

DATE: $ MAGIC MONEY DAY

Today I'm feeling ______

The exciting things I have in store for today are ______

______

Today's Magic Money™ mantra is ______

______

Today's Magic Money™ intention(s): It is so amazing that…

______

______

I bless ______ *as good, good, good!*

Today's Magic Money™ results include:

______

______

These magical things happened today…

______

DATE: $ MAGIC MONEY DAY

Today I'm feeling __________

The exciting things I have in store for today are __________

Today's Magic Money™ mantra is __________

Today's Magic Money™ intention(s): It is so amazing that…

I bless __________ *as good, good, good!*

Today's Magic Money™ results include:

These magical things happened today…

DATE: $ MAGIC MONEY DAY

Today I'm feeling __________

The exciting things I have in store for today are __________

Today's Magic Money™ mantra is __________

Today's Magic Money™ intention(s): It is so amazing that…

I bless __________ *as good, good, good!*

Today's Magic Money™ results include:

These magical things happened today…

DATE: $ MAGIC MONEY DAY

Today I'm feeling ______________________________

The exciting things I have in store for today are ______________________________

____

Today's Magic Money™ mantra is ______________________________

____

Today's Magic Money™ intention(s): It is so amazing that…

____

____

I bless ______________________________ *as good, good, good!*

Today's Magic Money™ results include:

____

____

These magical things happened today…

____

DATE: $ MAGIC MONEY DAY

Today I'm feeling ______________________________

The exciting things I have in store for today are ______________________________

____

Today's Magic Money™ mantra is ______________________________

____

Today's Magic Money™ intention(s): It is so amazing that…

____

____

I bless ______________________________ *as good, good, good!*

Today's Magic Money™ results include:

____

____

These magical things happened today…

____

DATE: $ MAGIC MONEY DAY

Today I'm feeling ______________________________

The exciting things I have in store for today are ______________________________

____

Today's Magic Money™ mantra is ______________________________

____

Today's Magic Money™ intention(s): It is so amazing that...

____

____

I bless ______________________________ *as good, good, good!*

Today's Magic Money™ results include:

____

____

These magical things happened today...

____

I practiced **Magic Money™ maximization** this week, and gave _____ %/$ to ________________ saved _____ %/$ in my opportunity chest, paid _____ %/$ for debt, put aside _____ %/$ for taxes and saved _____ %/$ for fun! It's going to be so fun to ______________________________

______________________________.

DATE: $ MAGIC MONEY DAY

Today I'm feeling __________

The exciting things I have in store for today are __________

Today's Magic Money™ mantra is __________

Today's Magic Money™ intention(s): It is so amazing that…

I bless __________ *as good, good, good!*

Today's Magic Money™ results include:

These magical things happened today…

DATE: $ MAGIC MONEY DAY

Today I'm feeling __________

The exciting things I have in store for today are __________

Today's Magic Money™ mantra is __________

Today's Magic Money™ intention(s): It is so amazing that…

I bless __________ *as good, good, good!*

Today's Magic Money™ results include:

These magical things happened today…

DATE: $ MAGIC MONEY DAY

Today I'm feeling ______

The exciting things I have in store for today are ______

______

Today's Magic Money™ mantra is ______

______

Today's Magic Money™ intention(s): It is so amazing that…

______

______

I bless ______ *as good, good, good!*

Today's Magic Money™ results include:

______

______

These magical things happened today…

______

DATE: $ MAGIC MONEY DAY

Today I'm feeling ______

The exciting things I have in store for today are ______

______

Today's Magic Money™ mantra is ______

______

Today's Magic Money™ intention(s): It is so amazing that…

______

______

I bless ______ *as good, good, good!*

Today's Magic Money™ results include:

______

______

These magical things happened today…

______

DATE: $ MAGIC MONEY DAY

Today I'm feeling ______

The exciting things I have in store for today are ______

______

Today's Magic Money™ mantra is ______

______

Today's Magic Money™ intention(s): It is so amazing that…

______

______

I bless ______ *as good, good, good!*

Today's Magic Money™ results include:

______

______

These magical things happened today…

______

DATE: $ MAGIC MONEY DAY

Today I'm feeling ______

The exciting things I have in store for today are ______

______

Today's Magic Money™ mantra is ______

______

Today's Magic Money™ intention(s): It is so amazing that…

______

______

I bless ______ *as good, good, good!*

Today's Magic Money™ results include:

______

______

These magical things happened today…

______

DATE: $ MAGIC MONEY DAY

Today I'm feeling ______

The exciting things I have in store for today are ______

______

Today's Magic Money™ mantra is ______

______

Today's Magic Money™ intention(s): It is so amazing that…

______

______

I bless ______ *as good, good, good!*

Today's Magic Money™ results include:

______

______

These magical things happened today…

______

I practiced **Magic Money™ maximization** this week, and gave _____ %/$ to ______ saved _____ %/$ in my opportunity chest, paid _____ %/$ for debt, put aside _____ %/$ for taxes and saved _____ %/$ for fun! It's going to be so fun to ______

______.

DATE: $ MAGIC MONEY DAY

Today I'm feeling ______

The exciting things I have in store for today are ______

______

Today's Magic Money™ mantra is ______

______

Today's Magic Money™ intention(s): It is so amazing that…

______

______

I bless ______ *as good, good, good!*

Today's Magic Money™ results include:

______

______

These magical things happened today…

______

DATE: $ MAGIC MONEY DAY

Today I'm feeling ______

The exciting things I have in store for today are ______

______

Today's Magic Money™ mantra is ______

______

Today's Magic Money™ intention(s): It is so amazing that…

______

______

I bless ______ *as good, good, good!*

Today's Magic Money™ results include:

______

______

These magical things happened today…

______

DATE: $ MAGIC MONEY DAY

Today I'm feeling ________________

The exciting things I have in store for today are ________________

Today's Magic Money™ mantra is ________________

Today's Magic Money™ intention(s): It is so amazing that…

I bless ________________ *as good, good, good!*

Today's Magic Money™ results include:

These magical things happened today…

DATE: $ MAGIC MONEY DAY

Today I'm feeling ________________

The exciting things I have in store for today are ________________

Today's Magic Money™ mantra is ________________

Today's Magic Money™ intention(s): It is so amazing that…

I bless ________________ *as good, good, good!*

Today's Magic Money™ results include:

These magical things happened today…

DATE: $ MAGIC MONEY DAY

Today I'm feeling ____________________

The exciting things I have in store for today are ____________________

Today's Magic Money™ mantra is ____________________

Today's Magic Money™ intention(s): It is so amazing that…

I bless ____________________ *as good, good, good!*

Today's Magic Money™ results include:

These magical things happened today…

DATE: $ MAGIC MONEY DAY

Today I'm feeling ____________________

The exciting things I have in store for today are ____________________

Today's Magic Money™ mantra is ____________________

Today's Magic Money™ intention(s): It is so amazing that…

I bless ____________________ *as good, good, good!*

Today's Magic Money™ results include:

These magical things happened today…

DATE: $ MAGIC MONEY DAY

Today I'm feeling ______________________________

The exciting things I have in store for today are ______________________________

____

Today's Magic Money™ mantra is ______________________________

____

Today's Magic Money™ intention(s): It is so amazing that…

____

____

I bless ______________________________ *as good, good, good!*

Today's Magic Money™ results include:

____

____

These magical things happened today…

____

I practiced **Magic Money™ maximization** this week, and gave _____ %/$ to __________________ saved _____ %/$ in my opportunity chest, paid _____ %/$ for debt, put aside _____ %/$ for taxes and saved _____ %/$ for fun! It's going to be so fun to ______________________________

______________________________.

DATE:	$	MAGIC MONEY DAY

Today I'm feeling ______________________________

The exciting things I have in store for today are ______________________________

____

Today's Magic Money™ mantra is ______________________________

____

Today's Magic Money™ intention(s): It is so amazing that…

____

____

I bless ______________________________ *as good, good, good!*

Today's Magic Money™ results include:

____

____

These magical things happened today…

____

DATE:	$	MAGIC MONEY DAY

Today I'm feeling ______________________________

The exciting things I have in store for today are ______________________________

____

Today's Magic Money™ mantra is ______________________________

____

Today's Magic Money™ intention(s): It is so amazing that…

____

____

I bless ______________________________ *as good, good, good!*

Today's Magic Money™ results include:

____

____

These magical things happened today…

____

DATE:	$	MAGIC MONEY DAY

Today I'm feeling ____________________

The exciting things I have in store for today are ____________________

____

Today's Magic Money™ mantra is ____________________

____

Today's Magic Money™ intention(s): It is so amazing that…

____

____

I bless ____________________ *as good, good, good!*

Today's Magic Money™ results include:

____

____

These magical things happened today…

____

DATE:	$	MAGIC MONEY DAY

Today I'm feeling ____________________

The exciting things I have in store for today are ____________________

____

Today's Magic Money™ mantra is ____________________

____

Today's Magic Money™ intention(s): It is so amazing that…

____

____

I bless ____________________ *as good, good, good!*

Today's Magic Money™ results include:

____

____

These magical things happened today…

____

DATE: $ MAGIC MONEY DAY

Today I'm feeling ______

The exciting things I have in store for today are ______

______

Today's Magic Money™ mantra is ______

______

Today's Magic Money™ intention(s): It is so amazing that…

______

______

I bless ______ *as good, good, good!*

Today's Magic Money™ results include:

______

______

These magical things happened today…

______

DATE: $ MAGIC MONEY DAY

Today I'm feeling ______

The exciting things I have in store for today are ______

______

Today's Magic Money™ mantra is ______

______

Today's Magic Money™ intention(s): It is so amazing that…

______

______

I bless ______ *as good, good, good!*

Today's Magic Money™ results include:

______

______

These magical things happened today…

______

DATE: $ MAGIC MONEY DAY

Today I'm feeling ______

The exciting things I have in store for today are ______

______

Today's Magic Money™ mantra is ______

______

Today's Magic Money™ intention(s): It is so amazing that…

______

______

I bless ______ *as good, good, good!*

Today's Magic Money™ results include:

______

______

These magical things happened today…

______

I practiced **Magic Money™ maximization** this week, and gave _____ %/$ to ______ saved _____ %/$ in my opportunity chest, paid _____ %/$ for debt, put aside _____ %/$ for taxes and saved _____ %/$ for fun! It's going to be so fun to ______

______.

DATE: $ MAGIC MONEY DAY

Today I'm feeling ____

The exciting things I have in store for today are __________________________

Today's Magic Money™ mantra is __________________________________

Today's Magic Money™ intention(s): It is so amazing that…

I bless ____________________________________ *as good, good, good!*

Today's Magic Money™ results include:

These magical things happened today…

DATE: $ MAGIC MONEY DAY

Today I'm feeling ____

The exciting things I have in store for today are __________________________

Today's Magic Money™ mantra is __________________________________

Today's Magic Money™ intention(s): It is so amazing that…

I bless ____________________________________ *as good, good, good!*

Today's Magic Money™ results include:

These magical things happened today…

DATE:	$	MAGIC MONEY DAY

Today I'm feeling ______________________________

The exciting things I have in store for today are ______________________________

____

Today's Magic Money™ mantra is ______________________________

____

Today's Magic Money™ intention(s): It is so amazing that…

____

____

I bless ______________________________ *as good, good, good!*

Today's Magic Money™ results include:

____

____

These magical things happened today…

____

DATE:	$	MAGIC MONEY DAY

Today I'm feeling ______________________________

The exciting things I have in store for today are ______________________________

____

Today's Magic Money™ mantra is ______________________________

____

Today's Magic Money™ intention(s): It is so amazing that…

____

____

I bless ______________________________ *as good, good, good!*

Today's Magic Money™ results include:

____

____

These magical things happened today…

____

DATE: $ MAGIC MONEY DAY

Today I'm feeling ______________________________

The exciting things I have in store for today are ______________________________

____

Today's Magic Money™ mantra is ______________________________

____

Today's Magic Money™ intention(s): It is so amazing that…

____

____

I bless ______________________________ *as good, good, good!*

Today's Magic Money™ results include:

____

____

These magical things happened today…

____

DATE: $ MAGIC MONEY DAY

Today I'm feeling ______________________________

The exciting things I have in store for today are ______________________________

____

Today's Magic Money™ mantra is ______________________________

____

Today's Magic Money™ intention(s): It is so amazing that…

____

____

I bless ______________________________ *as good, good, good!*

Today's Magic Money™ results include:

____

____

These magical things happened today…

____

DATE: $ MAGIC MONEY DAY

Today I'm feeling ______________________________

The exciting things I have in store for today are ______________________________

____

Today's Magic Money™ mantra is ______________________________

____

Today's Magic Money™ intention(s): It is so amazing that...

____

____

I bless ______________________________ *as good, good, good!*

Today's Magic Money™ results include:

____

____

These magical things happened today...

____

I practiced **Magic Money™ maximization** this week, and gave _____ %/$ to __________________ saved _____ %/$ in my opportunity chest, paid _____ %/$ for debt, put aside _____ %/$ for taxes and saved _____ %/$ for fun! It's going to be so fun to ______________________________

______________________________.

DATE: $ MAGIC MONEY DAY

Today I'm feeling ______

The exciting things I have in store for today are ______

Today's Magic Money™ mantra is ______

Today's Magic Money™ intention(s): It is so amazing that…

I bless ______ *as good, good, good!*

Today's Magic Money™ results include:

These magical things happened today…

DATE: $ MAGIC MONEY DAY

Today I'm feeling ______

The exciting things I have in store for today are ______

Today's Magic Money™ mantra is ______

Today's Magic Money™ intention(s): It is so amazing that…

I bless ______ *as good, good, good!*

Today's Magic Money™ results include:

These magical things happened today…

DATE: $ MAGIC MONEY DAY

Today I'm feeling ______

The exciting things I have in store for today are ______

______

Today's Magic Money™ mantra is ______

______

Today's Magic Money™ intention(s): It is so amazing that…

______

______

I bless ______ *as good, good, good!*

Today's Magic Money™ results include:

______

______

These magical things happened today…

______

DATE: $ MAGIC MONEY DAY

Today I'm feeling ______

The exciting things I have in store for today are ______

______

Today's Magic Money™ mantra is ______

______

Today's Magic Money™ intention(s): It is so amazing that…

______

______

I bless ______ *as good, good, good!*

Today's Magic Money™ results include:

______

______

These magical things happened today…

______

DATE: $ MAGIC MONEY DAY

Today I'm feeling ______

The exciting things I have in store for today are ______

______

Today's Magic Money™ mantra is ______

______

Today's Magic Money™ intention(s): It is so amazing that…

______

______

I bless ______ *as good, good, good!*

Today's Magic Money™ results include:

______

______

These magical things happened today…

______

DATE: $ MAGIC MONEY DAY

Today I'm feeling ______

The exciting things I have in store for today are ______

______

Today's Magic Money™ mantra is ______

______

Today's Magic Money™ intention(s): It is so amazing that…

______

______

I bless ______ *as good, good, good!*

Today's Magic Money™ results include:

______

______

These magical things happened today…

______

DATE: $ MAGIC MONEY DAY

Today I'm feeling ______________________________

The exciting things I have in store for today are ______________________________

____

Today's Magic Money™ mantra is ______________________________

____

Today's Magic Money™ intention(s): It is so amazing that…

____

____

I bless ______________________________ *as good, good, good!*

Today's Magic Money™ results include:

____

____

These magical things happened today…

____

I practiced **Magic Money™ maximization** this week, and gave _____ %/$ to __________________ saved _____ %/$ in my opportunity chest, paid _____ %/$ for debt, put aside _____ %/$ for taxes and saved _____ %/$ for fun! It's going to be so fun to ______________________________

______________________________.

DATE: $ MAGIC MONEY DAY

Today I'm feeling ______

The exciting things I have in store for today are ______

Today's Magic Money™ mantra is ______

Today's Magic Money™ intention(s): It is so amazing that…

I bless ______ *as good, good, good!*

Today's Magic Money™ results include:

These magical things happened today…

DATE: $ MAGIC MONEY DAY

Today I'm feeling ______

The exciting things I have in store for today are ______

Today's Magic Money™ mantra is ______

Today's Magic Money™ intention(s): It is so amazing that…

I bless ______ *as good, good, good!*

Today's Magic Money™ results include:

These magical things happened today…

DATE: $ MAGIC MONEY DAY

Today I'm feeling ______________________________

The exciting things I have in store for today are ______________________________

____

Today's Magic Money™ mantra is ______________________________

____

Today's Magic Money™ intention(s): It is so amazing that…

____

____

I bless ______________________________ *as good, good, good!*

Today's Magic Money™ results include:

____

____

These magical things happened today…

____

DATE: $ MAGIC MONEY DAY

Today I'm feeling ______________________________

The exciting things I have in store for today are ______________________________

____

Today's Magic Money™ mantra is ______________________________

____

Today's Magic Money™ intention(s): It is so amazing that…

____

____

I bless ______________________________ *as good, good, good!*

Today's Magic Money™ results include:

____

____

These magical things happened today…

____

DATE:	$	MAGIC MONEY DAY

Today I'm feeling ____________________

The exciting things I have in store for today are ____________________

Today's Magic Money™ mantra is ____________________

Today's Magic Money™ intention(s): It is so amazing that…

I bless ____________________ *as good, good, good!*

Today's Magic Money™ results include:

These magical things happened today…

DATE:	$	MAGIC MONEY DAY

Today I'm feeling ____________________

The exciting things I have in store for today are ____________________

Today's Magic Money™ mantra is ____________________

Today's Magic Money™ intention(s): It is so amazing that…

I bless ____________________ *as good, good, good!*

Today's Magic Money™ results include:

These magical things happened today…

DATE: $ MAGIC MONEY DAY

Today I'm feeling ______________________________

The exciting things I have in store for today are ______________________________

____

Today's Magic Money™ mantra is ______________________________

____

Today's Magic Money™ intention(s): It is so amazing that…

____

____

I bless ______________________________ *as good, good, good!*

Today's Magic Money™ results include:

____

____

These magical things happened today…

____

I practiced **Magic Money™ maximization** this week, and gave _____ %/$ to __________________ saved _____ %/$ in my opportunity chest, paid _____ %/$ for debt, put aside _____ %/$ for taxes and saved _____ %/$ for fun! It's going to be so fun to ______________________________

______________________________.

DATE: $ MAGIC MONEY DAY

Today I'm feeling ____________________

The exciting things I have in store for today are ____________________

____

Today's Magic Money™ mantra is ____________________

____

Today's Magic Money™ intention(s): It is so amazing that...

____

____

I bless ____________________ *as good, good, good!*

Today's Magic Money™ results include:

____

____

These magical things happened today...

____

DATE: $ MAGIC MONEY DAY

Today I'm feeling ____________________

The exciting things I have in store for today are ____________________

____

Today's Magic Money™ mantra is ____________________

____

Today's Magic Money™ intention(s): It is so amazing that...

____

____

I bless ____________________ *as good, good, good!*

Today's Magic Money™ results include:

____

____

These magical things happened today...

____

DATE:	$	MAGIC MONEY DAY

Today I'm feeling ______________________________

The exciting things I have in store for today are ______________________________

____

Today's Magic Money™ mantra is ______________________________

____

Today's Magic Money™ intention(s): It is so amazing that…

____

____

I bless ______________________________ *as good, good, good!*

Today's Magic Money™ results include:

____

____

These magical things happened today…

____

DATE:	$	MAGIC MONEY DAY

Today I'm feeling ______________________________

The exciting things I have in store for today are ______________________________

____

Today's Magic Money™ mantra is ______________________________

____

Today's Magic Money™ intention(s): It is so amazing that…

____

____

I bless ______________________________ *as good, good, good!*

Today's Magic Money™ results include:

____

____

These magical things happened today…

____

DATE: $ MAGIC MONEY DAY

Today I'm feeling ______

The exciting things I have in store for today are ______

Today's Magic Money™ mantra is ______

Today's Magic Money™ intention(s): It is so amazing that…

I bless ______ *as good, good, good!*

Today's Magic Money™ results include:

These magical things happened today…

DATE: $ MAGIC MONEY DAY

Today I'm feeling ______

The exciting things I have in store for today are ______

Today's Magic Money™ mantra is ______

Today's Magic Money™ intention(s): It is so amazing that…

I bless ______ *as good, good, good!*

Today's Magic Money™ results include:

These magical things happened today…

DATE: $ MAGIC MONEY DAY

Today I'm feeling ____________________

The exciting things I have in store for today are ____________________

____

Today's Magic Money™ mantra is ____________________

____

Today's Magic Money™ intention(s): It is so amazing that…

____

____

I bless ____________________ *as good, good, good!*

Today's Magic Money™ results include:

____

____

These magical things happened today…

____

I practiced **Magic Money™ maximization** this week, and gave _____ %/$ to __________ saved _____ %/$ in my opportunity chest, paid _____ %/$ for debt, put aside _____ %/$ for taxes and saved _____ %/$ for fun! It's going to be so fun to ____________________

____________________.

DATE: $ MAGIC MONEY DAY

Today I'm feeling ______

The exciting things I have in store for today are ______

______

Today's Magic Money™ mantra is ______

______

Today's Magic Money™ intention(s): It is so amazing that…

______

______

I bless ______ *as good, good, good!*

Today's Magic Money™ results include:

______

______

These magical things happened today…

______

DATE: $ MAGIC MONEY DAY

Today I'm feeling ______

The exciting things I have in store for today are ______

______

Today's Magic Money™ mantra is ______

______

Today's Magic Money™ intention(s): It is so amazing that…

______

______

I bless ______ *as good, good, good!*

Today's Magic Money™ results include:

______

______

These magical things happened today…

______

DATE: $ MAGIC MONEY DAY

Today I'm feeling __________

The exciting things I have in store for today are __________

Today's Magic Money™ mantra is __________

Today's Magic Money™ intention(s): It is so amazing that…

I bless __________ *as good, good, good!*

Today's Magic Money™ results include:

These magical things happened today…

DATE: $ MAGIC MONEY DAY

Today I'm feeling __________

The exciting things I have in store for today are __________

Today's Magic Money™ mantra is __________

Today's Magic Money™ intention(s): It is so amazing that…

I bless __________ *as good, good, good!*

Today's Magic Money™ results include:

These magical things happened today…

DATE: $ MAGIC MONEY DAY

Today I'm feeling ______

The exciting things I have in store for today are ______

______

Today's Magic Money™ mantra is ______

______

Today's Magic Money™ intention(s): It is so amazing that…

______

______

I bless ______ *as good, good, good!*

Today's Magic Money™ results include:

______

______

These magical things happened today…

______

DATE: $ MAGIC MONEY DAY

Today I'm feeling ______

The exciting things I have in store for today are ______

______

Today's Magic Money™ mantra is ______

______

Today's Magic Money™ intention(s): It is so amazing that…

______

______

I bless ______ *as good, good, good!*

Today's Magic Money™ results include:

______

______

These magical things happened today…

______

DATE:	$	MAGIC MONEY DAY

Today I'm feeling ______________________________

The exciting things I have in store for today are ______________________________

____

Today's Magic Money™ mantra is ______________________________

____

Today's Magic Money™ intention(s): It is so amazing that…

____

____

I bless ______________________________ *as good, good, good!*

Today's Magic Money™ results include:

____

____

These magical things happened today…

____

I practiced **Magic Money™ maximization** this week, and gave _____ %/$ to _________________ saved _____ %/$ in my opportunity chest, paid _____ %/$ for debt, put aside _____ %/$ for taxes and saved _____ %/$ for fun! It's going to be so fun to ______________________________

______________________________.

DATE: $ MAGIC MONEY DAY

Today I'm feeling ______

The exciting things I have in store for today are ______

Today's Magic Money™ mantra is ______

Today's Magic Money™ intention(s): It is so amazing that…

I bless ______ *as good, good, good!*

Today's Magic Money™ results include:

These magical things happened today…

DATE: $ MAGIC MONEY DAY

Today I'm feeling ______

The exciting things I have in store for today are ______

Today's Magic Money™ mantra is ______

Today's Magic Money™ intention(s): It is so amazing that…

I bless ______ *as good, good, good!*

Today's Magic Money™ results include:

These magical things happened today…

DATE: $ MAGIC MONEY DAY

Today I'm feeling ______

The exciting things I have in store for today are ______

Today's Magic Money™ mantra is ______

Today's Magic Money™ intention(s): It is so amazing that…

I bless ______ *as good, good, good!*

Today's Magic Money™ results include:

These magical things happened today…

DATE: $ MAGIC MONEY DAY

Today I'm feeling ______

The exciting things I have in store for today are ______

Today's Magic Money™ mantra is ______

Today's Magic Money™ intention(s): It is so amazing that…

I bless ______ *as good, good, good!*

Today's Magic Money™ results include:

These magical things happened today…

DATE: $ MAGIC MONEY DAY

Today I'm feeling ______

The exciting things I have in store for today are ______

Today's Magic Money™ mantra is ______

Today's Magic Money™ intention(s): It is so amazing that...

I bless ______ *as good, good, good!*

Today's Magic Money™ results include:

These magical things happened today...

DATE: $ MAGIC MONEY DAY

Today I'm feeling ______

The exciting things I have in store for today are ______

Today's Magic Money™ mantra is ______

Today's Magic Money™ intention(s): It is so amazing that...

I bless ______ *as good, good, good!*

Today's Magic Money™ results include:

These magical things happened today...

DATE: $ MAGIC MONEY DAY

Today I'm feeling ______________________________

The exciting things I have in store for today are ______________________________

____

Today's Magic Money™ mantra is ______________________________

____

Today's Magic Money™ intention(s): It is so amazing that…

____

____

I bless ______________________________ *as good, good, good!*

Today's Magic Money™ results include:

____

____

These magical things happened today…

____

I practiced **Magic Money™ maximization** this week, and gave _____ %/$ to __________ saved _____ %/$ in my opportunity chest, paid _____ %/$ for debt, put aside _____ %/$ for taxes and saved _____ %/$ for fun! It's going to be so fun to ______________________________

______________________________.

DATE: $ MAGIC MONEY DAY

Today I'm feeling ___

The exciting things I have in store for today are ___

Today's Magic Money™ mantra is ___

Today's Magic Money™ intention(s): It is so amazing that…

I bless ___ *as good, good, good!*

Today's Magic Money™ results include:

These magical things happened today…

DATE: $ MAGIC MONEY DAY

Today I'm feeling ___

The exciting things I have in store for today are ___

Today's Magic Money™ mantra is ___

Today's Magic Money™ intention(s): It is so amazing that…

I bless ___ *as good, good, good!*

Today's Magic Money™ results include:

These magical things happened today…

DATE: $ MAGIC MONEY DAY

Today I'm feeling ______

The exciting things I have in store for today are ______

______

Today's Magic Money™ mantra is ______

______

Today's Magic Money™ intention(s): It is so amazing that…

______

______

I bless ______ *as good, good, good!*

Today's Magic Money™ results include:

______

______

These magical things happened today…

______

DATE: $ MAGIC MONEY DAY

Today I'm feeling ______

The exciting things I have in store for today are ______

______

Today's Magic Money™ mantra is ______

______

Today's Magic Money™ intention(s): It is so amazing that…

______

______

I bless ______ *as good, good, good!*

Today's Magic Money™ results include:

______

______

These magical things happened today…

______

DATE: $ MAGIC MONEY DAY

Today I'm feeling ______

The exciting things I have in store for today are ______

Today's Magic Money™ mantra is ______

Today's Magic Money™ intention(s): It is so amazing that…

I bless ______ *as good, good, good!*

Today's Magic Money™ results include:

These magical things happened today…

DATE: $ MAGIC MONEY DAY

Today I'm feeling ______

The exciting things I have in store for today are ______

Today's Magic Money™ mantra is ______

Today's Magic Money™ intention(s): It is so amazing that…

I bless ______ *as good, good, good!*

Today's Magic Money™ results include:

These magical things happened today…

DATE:	$	MAGIC MONEY DAY

Today I'm feeling ______________________________

The exciting things I have in store for today are ______________________________

____

Today's Magic Money™ mantra is ______________________________

____

Today's Magic Money™ intention(s): It is so amazing that…

____

____

I bless ______________________________ *as good, good, good!*

Today's Magic Money™ results include:

____

____

These magical things happened today…

____

I practiced **Magic Money™ maximization** this week, and gave _____ %/$ to _________________ saved _____ %/$ in my opportunity chest, paid _____ %/$ for debt, put aside _____ %/$ for taxes and saved _____ %/$ for fun! It's going to be so fun to ______________________________

______________________________.

DATE: $ MAGIC MONEY DAY

Today I'm feeling ______

The exciting things I have in store for today are ______

______

Today's Magic Money™ mantra is ______

______

Today's Magic Money™ intention(s): It is so amazing that…

______

______

I bless ______ *as good, good, good!*

Today's Magic Money™ results include:

______

______

These magical things happened today…

______

DATE: $ MAGIC MONEY DAY

Today I'm feeling ______

The exciting things I have in store for today are ______

______

Today's Magic Money™ mantra is ______

______

Today's Magic Money™ intention(s): It is so amazing that…

______

______

I bless ______ *as good, good, good!*

Today's Magic Money™ results include:

______

______

These magical things happened today…

______

DATE: $ MAGIC MONEY DAY

Today I'm feeling __________

The exciting things I have in store for today are __________

Today's Magic Money™ mantra is __________

Today's Magic Money™ intention(s): It is so amazing that…

I bless __________ *as good, good, good!*

Today's Magic Money™ results include:

These magical things happened today…

DATE: $ MAGIC MONEY DAY

Today I'm feeling __________

The exciting things I have in store for today are __________

Today's Magic Money™ mantra is __________

Today's Magic Money™ intention(s): It is so amazing that…

I bless __________ *as good, good, good!*

Today's Magic Money™ results include:

These magical things happened today…

DATE: $ MAGIC MONEY DAY

Today I'm feeling ______

The exciting things I have in store for today are ______

______

Today's Magic Money™ mantra is ______

______

Today's Magic Money™ intention(s): It is so amazing that…

______

______

I bless ______ *as good, good, good!*

Today's Magic Money™ results include:

______

______

These magical things happened today…

______

DATE: $ MAGIC MONEY DAY

Today I'm feeling ______

The exciting things I have in store for today are ______

______

Today's Magic Money™ mantra is ______

______

Today's Magic Money™ intention(s): It is so amazing that…

______

______

I bless ______ *as good, good, good!*

Today's Magic Money™ results include:

______

______

These magical things happened today…

______

DATE: $ MAGIC MONEY DAY

Today I'm feeling ____________________

The exciting things I have in store for today are ____________________

____

Today's Magic Money™ mantra is ____________________

____

Today's Magic Money™ intention(s): It is so amazing that…

____

____

I bless ____________________ *as good, good, good!*

Today's Magic Money™ results include:

____

____

These magical things happened today…

____

I practiced **Magic Money™ maximization** this week, and gave _____ %/$ to ________________ saved _____ %/$ in my opportunity chest, paid _____ %/$ for debt, put aside _____ %/$ for taxes and saved _____ %/$ for fun! It's going to be so fun to ____________________

____________________.

DATE: $ MAGIC MONEY DAY

Today I'm feeling ____________________

The exciting things I have in store for today are ____________________

Today's Magic Money™ mantra is ____________________

Today's Magic Money™ intention(s): It is so amazing that…

I bless ____________________ *as good, good, good!*

Today's Magic Money™ results include:

These magical things happened today…

DATE: $ MAGIC MONEY DAY

Today I'm feeling ____________________

The exciting things I have in store for today are ____________________

Today's Magic Money™ mantra is ____________________

Today's Magic Money™ intention(s): It is so amazing that…

I bless ____________________ *as good, good, good!*

Today's Magic Money™ results include:

These magical things happened today…

DATE: $ MAGIC MONEY DAY

Today I'm feeling ______

The exciting things I have in store for today are ______

Today's Magic Money™ mantra is ______

Today's Magic Money™ intention(s): It is so amazing that…

I bless ______ *as good, good, good!*

Today's Magic Money™ results include:

These magical things happened today…

DATE: $ MAGIC MONEY DAY

Today I'm feeling ______

The exciting things I have in store for today are ______

Today's Magic Money™ mantra is ______

Today's Magic Money™ intention(s): It is so amazing that…

I bless ______ *as good, good, good!*

Today's Magic Money™ results include:

These magical things happened today…

DATE: $ MAGIC MONEY DAY

Today I'm feeling ______

The exciting things I have in store for today are ______

______

Today's Magic Money™ mantra is ______

______

Today's Magic Money™ intention(s): It is so amazing that…

______

______

I bless ______ *as good, good, good!*

Today's Magic Money™ results include:

______

______

These magical things happened today…

______

DATE: $ MAGIC MONEY DAY

Today I'm feeling ______

The exciting things I have in store for today are ______

______

Today's Magic Money™ mantra is ______

______

Today's Magic Money™ intention(s): It is so amazing that…

______

______

I bless ______ *as good, good, good!*

Today's Magic Money™ results include:

______

______

These magical things happened today…

______

DATE: $ MAGIC MONEY DAY

Today I'm feeling ______________________________

The exciting things I have in store for today are ______________________________

____

Today's Magic Money™ mantra is ______________________________

____

Today's Magic Money™ intention(s): It is so amazing that…

____

____

I bless ______________________________ *as good, good, good!*

Today's Magic Money™ results include:

____

____

These magical things happened today…

____

I practiced **Magic Money™ maximization** this week, and gave _____ %/$ to __________________ saved _____ %/$ in my opportunity chest, paid _____ %/$ for debt, put aside _____ %/$ for taxes and saved _____ %/$ for fun! It's going to be so fun to ______________________________

______________________________.

DATE: $ MAGIC MONEY DAY

Today I'm feeling ______

The exciting things I have in store for today are ______

______

Today's Magic Money™ mantra is ______

______

Today's Magic Money™ intention(s): It is so amazing that…

______

______

I bless ______ *as good, good, good!*

Today's Magic Money™ results include:

______

______

These magical things happened today…

______

DATE: $ MAGIC MONEY DAY

Today I'm feeling ______

The exciting things I have in store for today are ______

______

Today's Magic Money™ mantra is ______

______

Today's Magic Money™ intention(s): It is so amazing that…

______

______

I bless ______ *as good, good, good!*

Today's Magic Money™ results include:

______

______

These magical things happened today…

______

DATE: $ MAGIC MONEY DAY

Today I'm feeling ____________________

The exciting things I have in store for today are ____________________

*Today's Magic Money™ mantra is*____________________

Today's Magic Money™ intention(s): It is so amazing that…

I bless ____________________*as good, good, good!*

Today's Magic Money™ results include:

These magical things happened today…

DATE: $ MAGIC MONEY DAY

Today I'm feeling ____________________

The exciting things I have in store for today are ____________________

*Today's Magic Money™ mantra is*____________________

Today's Magic Money™ intention(s): It is so amazing that…

I bless ____________________*as good, good, good!*

Today's Magic Money™ results include:

These magical things happened today…

DATE: $ MAGIC MONEY DAY

Today I'm feeling ______

The exciting things I have in store for today are ______

______

Today's Magic Money™ mantra is ______

______

Today's Magic Money™ intention(s): It is so amazing that...

______

______

I bless ______ *as good, good, good!*

Today's Magic Money™ results include:

______

______

These magical things happened today...

______

DATE: $ MAGIC MONEY DAY

Today I'm feeling ______

The exciting things I have in store for today are ______

______

Today's Magic Money™ mantra is ______

______

Today's Magic Money™ intention(s): It is so amazing that...

______

______

I bless ______ *as good, good, good!*

Today's Magic Money™ results include:

______

______

These magical things happened today...

______

DATE: $ MAGIC MONEY DAY

Today I'm feeling ____________________

The exciting things I have in store for today are ____________________

____

Today's Magic Money™ mantra is ____________________

____

Today's Magic Money™ intention(s): It is so amazing that…

____

____

I bless ____________________ *as good, good, good!*

Today's Magic Money™ results include:

____

____

These magical things happened today…

____

I practiced **Magic Money™ maximization** this week, and gave _____ %/$ to ________________ saved _____ %/$ in my opportunity chest, paid _____ %/$ for debt, put aside _____ %/$ for taxes and saved _____ %/$ for fun! It's going to be so fun to ____________________ ____________________.

DATE: $ MAGIC MONEY DAY

Today I'm feeling ______

The exciting things I have in store for today are ______

______

Today's Magic Money™ mantra is ______

______

Today's Magic Money™ intention(s): It is so amazing that…

______

______

I bless ______ *as good, good, good!*

Today's Magic Money™ results include:

______

______

These magical things happened today…

______

DATE: $ MAGIC MONEY DAY

Today I'm feeling ______

The exciting things I have in store for today are ______

______

Today's Magic Money™ mantra is ______

______

Today's Magic Money™ intention(s): It is so amazing that…

______

______

I bless ______ *as good, good, good!*

Today's Magic Money™ results include:

______

______

These magical things happened today…

______

DATE:	$	MAGIC MONEY DAY

Today I'm feeling ____________________

The exciting things I have in store for today are ____________________

Today's Magic Money™ mantra is ____________________

Today's Magic Money™ intention(s): It is so amazing that…

I bless ____________________ *as good, good, good!*

Today's Magic Money™ results include:

These magical things happened today…

DATE:	$	MAGIC MONEY DAY

Today I'm feeling ____________________

The exciting things I have in store for today are ____________________

Today's Magic Money™ mantra is ____________________

Today's Magic Money™ intention(s): It is so amazing that…

I bless ____________________ *as good, good, good!*

Today's Magic Money™ results include:

These magical things happened today…

DATE:	$	MAGIC MONEY DAY

Today I'm feeling ____________________

The exciting things I have in store for today are ____________________

____

Today's Magic Money™ mantra is ____________________

____

Today's Magic Money™ intention(s): It is so amazing that…

____

____

I bless ____________________ *as good, good, good!*

Today's Magic Money™ results include:

____

____

These magical things happened today…

____

DATE:	$	MAGIC MONEY DAY

Today I'm feeling ____________________

The exciting things I have in store for today are ____________________

____

Today's Magic Money™ mantra is ____________________

____

Today's Magic Money™ intention(s): It is so amazing that…

____

____

I bless ____________________ *as good, good, good!*

Today's Magic Money™ results include:

____

____

These magical things happened today…

____

DATE: $ MAGIC MONEY DAY

Today I'm feeling ________________________________

The exciting things I have in store for today are ________________________________

____

Today's Magic Money™ mantra is ________________________________

____

Today's Magic Money™ intention(s): It is so amazing that…

____

____

I bless ________________________________ *as good, good, good!*

Today's Magic Money™ results include:

____

____

These magical things happened today…

____

I practiced **Magic Money™ maximization** this week, and gave _____ %/$ to ________________ saved _____ %/$ in my opportunity chest, paid _____ %/$ for debt, put aside _____ %/$ for taxes and saved _____ %/$ for fun! It's going to be so fun to ________________________________

________________________________.

DATE: $ MAGIC MONEY DAY

Today I'm feeling __________

The exciting things I have in store for today are __________

Today's Magic Money™ mantra is __________

Today's Magic Money™ intention(s): It is so amazing that…

I bless __________ *as good, good, good!*

Today's Magic Money™ results include:

These magical things happened today…

DATE: $ MAGIC MONEY DAY

Today I'm feeling __________

The exciting things I have in store for today are __________

Today's Magic Money™ mantra is __________

Today's Magic Money™ intention(s): It is so amazing that…

I bless __________ *as good, good, good!*

Today's Magic Money™ results include:

These magical things happened today…

DATE: $ MAGIC MONEY DAY

Today I'm feeling ____

The exciting things I have in store for today are ________________________________

____

Today's Magic Money™ mantra is ____

____

Today's Magic Money™ intention(s): It is so amazing that…

____

____

I bless ____ *as good, good, good!*

Today's Magic Money™ results include:

____

____

These magical things happened today…

____

DATE: $ MAGIC MONEY DAY

Today I'm feeling ____

The exciting things I have in store for today are ________________________________

____

Today's Magic Money™ mantra is ____

____

Today's Magic Money™ intention(s): It is so amazing that…

____

____

I bless ____ *as good, good, good!*

Today's Magic Money™ results include:

____

____

These magical things happened today…

____

DATE: $ MAGIC MONEY DAY

Today I'm feeling ______

The exciting things I have in store for today are ______

Today's Magic Money™ mantra is ______

Today's Magic Money™ intention(s): It is so amazing that…

I bless ______ *as good, good, good!*

Today's Magic Money™ results include:

These magical things happened today…

DATE: $ MAGIC MONEY DAY

Today I'm feeling ______

The exciting things I have in store for today are ______

Today's Magic Money™ mantra is ______

Today's Magic Money™ intention(s): It is so amazing that…

I bless ______ *as good, good, good!*

Today's Magic Money™ results include:

These magical things happened today…

DATE:	$	MAGIC MONEY DAY

Today I'm feeling ______________________________

The exciting things I have in store for today are ______________________________

____

Today's Magic Money™ mantra is ______________________________

____

Today's Magic Money™ intention(s): It is so amazing that…

____

____

I bless ______________________________ *as good, good, good!*

Today's Magic Money™ results include:

____

____

These magical things happened today…

____

I practiced **Magic Money**™ **maximization** this week, and gave _____ %/$ to _________________ saved _____ %/$ in my opportunity chest, paid _____ %/$ for debt, put aside _____ %/$ for taxes and saved _____ %/$ for fun! It's going to be so fun to ______________________________

______________________________.

DATE: $ MAGIC MONEY DAY

Today I'm feeling ____________________

The exciting things I have in store for today are ____________________

____

Today's Magic Money™ mantra is ____________________

____

Today's Magic Money™ intention(s): It is so amazing that…

____

____

I bless ____________________ *as good, good, good!*

Today's Magic Money™ results include:

____

____

These magical things happened today…

____

DATE: $ MAGIC MONEY DAY

Today I'm feeling ____________________

The exciting things I have in store for today are ____________________

____

Today's Magic Money™ mantra is ____________________

____

Today's Magic Money™ intention(s): It is so amazing that…

____

____

I bless ____________________ *as good, good, good!*

Today's Magic Money™ results include:

____

____

These magical things happened today…

____

DATE:	$	MAGIC MONEY DAY

Today I'm feeling ______

The exciting things I have in store for today are ______

______

Today's Magic Money™ mantra is ______

______

Today's Magic Money™ intention(s): It is so amazing that…

______

______

I bless ______ *as good, good, good!*

Today's Magic Money™ results include:

______

______

These magical things happened today…

______

DATE:	$	MAGIC MONEY DAY

Today I'm feeling ______

The exciting things I have in store for today are ______

______

Today's Magic Money™ mantra is ______

______

Today's Magic Money™ intention(s): It is so amazing that…

______

______

I bless ______ *as good, good, good!*

Today's Magic Money™ results include:

______

______

These magical things happened today…

______

DATE: $ MAGIC MONEY DAY

Today I'm feeling ______

The exciting things I have in store for today are ______

______

Today's Magic Money™ mantra is ______

______

Today's Magic Money™ intention(s): It is so amazing that…

______

______

I bless ______ *as good, good, good!*

Today's Magic Money™ results include:

______

______

These magical things happened today…

______

DATE: $ MAGIC MONEY DAY

Today I'm feeling ______

The exciting things I have in store for today are ______

______

Today's Magic Money™ mantra is ______

______

Today's Magic Money™ intention(s): It is so amazing that…

______

______

I bless ______ *as good, good, good!*

Today's Magic Money™ results include:

______

______

These magical things happened today…

______

DATE:	$	MAGIC MONEY DAY

Today I'm feeling ______________________________

The exciting things I have in store for today are ______________________________

____

Today's Magic Money™ mantra is ______________________________

____

Today's Magic Money™ intention(s): It is so amazing that…

____

____

I bless ______________________________ *as good, good, good!*

Today's Magic Money™ results include:

____

____

These magical things happened today…

____

I practiced **Magic Money™ maximization** this week, and gave _____ %/$ to __________________ saved _____ %/$ in my opportunity chest, paid _____ %/$ for debt, put aside _____ %/$ for taxes and saved _____ %/$ for fun! It's going to be so fun to ______________________________

______________________________.

DATE: $ MAGIC MONEY DAY

Today I'm feeling ______

The exciting things I have in store for today are ______

______

Today's Magic Money™ mantra is ______

______

Today's Magic Money™ intention(s): It is so amazing that…

______

______

I bless ______ *as good, good, good!*

Today's Magic Money™ results include:

______

______

These magical things happened today…

______

DATE: $ MAGIC MONEY DAY

Today I'm feeling ______

The exciting things I have in store for today are ______

______

Today's Magic Money™ mantra is ______

______

Today's Magic Money™ intention(s): It is so amazing that…

______

______

I bless ______ *as good, good, good!*

Today's Magic Money™ results include:

______

______

These magical things happened today…

______

DATE: $ MAGIC MONEY DAY

Today I'm feeling ______

The exciting things I have in store for today are ______

Today's Magic Money™ mantra is ______

Today's Magic Money™ intention(s): It is so amazing that…

I bless ______ *as good, good, good!*

Today's Magic Money™ results include:

These magical things happened today…

DATE: $ MAGIC MONEY DAY

Today I'm feeling ______

The exciting things I have in store for today are ______

Today's Magic Money™ mantra is ______

Today's Magic Money™ intention(s): It is so amazing that…

I bless ______ *as good, good, good!*

Today's Magic Money™ results include:

These magical things happened today…

DATE: $ MAGIC MONEY DAY

Today I'm feeling ____________________

The exciting things I have in store for today are ____________________

Today's Magic Money™ mantra is ____________________

Today's Magic Money™ intention(s): It is so amazing that…

I bless ____________________ *as good, good, good!*

Today's Magic Money™ results include:

These magical things happened today…

I practiced **Magic Money™ maximization** this week, and gave _____ %/$ to __________________ saved _____ %/$ in my opportunity chest, paid _____ %/$ for debt, put aside _____ %/$ for taxes and saved _____ %/$ for fun! It's going to be so fun to ____.

THE MAGIC MONEY PROJECT

Not long after I published the *Magic Money* books, I received a Facebook message from Joe Carlisle. He asked if he could do his own group and conduct a 365-day experiment with the Magic Money™ philosophy. My reply: *Of course!* I highly encourage you to join both the Magic Money™ Facebook and Magic Money™ Project Facebook groups. You'll love Joe's group because he posts daily videos that share his progress, challenges, and aha moments.

Joe is now famous for creating a fun acronym: UHORU, based on the first Magic Money™ experiment. It stands for "remain Unmoved, Hand it Over (to God/the Universe) and Remain Unattached. Whenever you're experiencing a challenge (a setback, unexpected bill, a delay or a denial), just say "UHORU!" and after you're finished laughing hysterically, keep in mind the best is yet to come.

I asked Joe to share his favorite mantras and here's the list he sent. I hope they are helpful for you!

- Magic Money™ is easy!
- I am a money magnet!
- I attract money in ever increasing amounts.
- I attract opportunities and ideas that increase my wealth and abundance.
- Money flows freely to me in ever increasing amounts, in freaky abundance, from both expected and unexpected sources.
- Money loves me, and I love and respect my money.
- Money comes to me from everywhere all the time.
- I only speak and think about money positively and with respect.
- I am open to money coming to me from anywhere at any time.
- Money comes to me from anywhere at any time.
- There is more than enough money and everything else for me now and henceforth forever.
- An abundance of everything I need is on its way to me right now.
- I take power over my life by choosing with intent and purpose to create a life better than I have ever had before.

- My best, most wealthy and financially secure years are in front of me
- Money just finds its way to me always and everywhere.
- I find money everywhere I go.
- I always have—and attract—great money-making ideas, inspiration, and opportunities.
- Delays are good, disappointment is only temporary.
- Money is constantly flowing to me, even when I don't see or perceive it.
- Magic Money™ is peacefully achieved and received.
- I understand and practice the Magic Money™ philosophy in all my affairs.
- I live in abundance and always have enough for all my needs and whatever else I may want.
- My finances are stable, I spend my money with intent and purpose, and I feel secure.
- I am committed to the Magic Money™ philosophy and its process.
- I release Magic Money™ to work in my life.

MAGIC MONEY MANTRAS

These, and all of my #MagicMoneyMantras, have been inspired by Catherine Ponder, Florence Scovel Shinn, Stuart Wilde, Eric Butterworth, Ernest Holmes, and even Tony Robbins. I give thanks to these mentors who have inspired me, and I hope these mantras, in turn, inspire you.

I suggest you spend time every day contemplating the Universal abundance available to you, and give thanks it massively appears in your life. Ask for help about anything that concerns you and allow what you need to come to you.

You can put these, and other, #MagicMoneyMantras on 3 x 5" or 4 x 6" cards (a few are ready for you to cut-out at the back of this journal) and put them on your bathroom mirror and/or in your car (along with writing them in your Magic Money™ journal). Say them while you brush your teeth, at traffic lights, or while you wait for someone.

Remember: You can change God to the Universe or vice versa. Whatever works for you.

One final thought: use the mantras, below, as inspiration to create your own! Make sure they are:

- *Positive*
- *Future-focused*
- *...and don't contain any negative words.*

Without further ado, here are my mantras:

1. As money goes out, immediately DOUBLE the money comes in! (*I say this whenever I pay any bill or spend money in any capacity.*)
2. I am a money magnet! I receive money every single day! I have soooooo much money!
3. My wallet and bank accounts are always crammed and jammed with abundance, under grace, in perfect ways.
4. My good is at hand and it quickly appears now, in multiple ways, for my personal use, and I use it wisely!
5. My good wants me as much as I want it! All the good that I have not recognized or claimed in the past has not been lost. It has been dammed-up in the invisible, and I claim it now! The good that was not claimed in the past is still mine, and I am receiving it now!

6. Massive wealth is circulating in my life. It flows to me in avalanches of abundance. All of my needs, goals, and desires are now met instantaneously, for I am one with God and God is everything.!
7. I give thanks my world is full of charming people who now lovingly help me in every way.
8. Large sums of money, big happy financial surprises, and rich amazing gifts now come to me, under grace, in perfect ways!
9. Every day in every way I am growing more and more financially prosperous now!
10. I give thanks for a large, steady, dependable permanent financial income now!

This is one of my very favorite #MagicMoneyMantras:

I am wonderful and I love myself. THIS is one of the best days of my life! Everything is working out for my highest good. Whatever I need to know now is revealed to me. Whatever I need comes to me. All is well.

I love it because it covers everything. It points my focus forward and positively so. It increases my peace of mind and reduces any anxiety I might be feeling. For a long time, I had it on a 3 x 5" card and carried it around in my wallet. Even though I rarely have any negative energy around money or finances any more, I still say it on the regular.

Why? Because I don't want to stop that #MagicMoneyFlow!

What's YOUR favorite Magic Money™ Mantra?

____

____

____

Remember: Bless everything as good, good, good!

Take your purse, wallet and/or checkbook into your hands and give it a #MagicMoneyBlessing:

I bless you and bless you with abundant gratitude for the riches of God (the Universe) that are now being demonstrated for me in you and through you.

You can also say this mantra every day:

I bless persons and conditions as channels of my prosperity, but God (the Universe) is the Source of my supply. God (the Universe) provides His (its) own amazing channels of supply to me now!

BLESSINGS

Sometimes (sometimes) when Magic Money™ is slow to come, it is because we're holding on too tight to a grudge or hurt or anger or frustration toward a person, situation, event, or thing. And yes, I talk about taking full responsibility for everything and blessing everything as good.

BUT!

Every so often, there's one thing in particular that stays in our minds or hearts. It happened to me just the other day. When I remembered someone I hadn't seen in a couple of years, who at Christmastime had done something that can only be termed as "sh*tty," I realized I had some forgiveness left to give and some blessing to do.

My first thought was, "Aww, man; I'm still mad and resentful. Better get that cleared out!"

So, I spent some extra time in my Magic Money™ journal and the whole day saying their name, and "I bless you and bless you for all of the goodness of God that is working in you and through you. I bless you as good, good, good!" I also said, "I fully, freely forgive you, and bless you with your highest good now."

(Yes, you can substitute Universe with God.)

I said it OVER and OVER until I felt neutral about that person. Then, I kept saying it until when I thought about them, I started to remember a few fun times we had and laughs we shared.

Forgiveness and blessing aren't ever about anyone but ourselves. Being mad or hurt or unforgiving (or all of them!) is like drinking poison and expecting someone else to die.

Please, if you have anyone against whom you hold any negative feelings, give YOURSELF the gift of blessing and forgiveness. These pages are for you to write blessings towards those people, places, and things causing you angst.

P.S. You're only human. It may take time and a few thousand mantras before you really feel it.

I bless ____________________________________ as good, good, good.

____

____

____

THE MAGIC MONEY MINUTE

We're all busy—running a million miles an hour, sometimes juggling spouses, kids, work, the holidays, volunteering, extra projects, and hobbies.

Whew!

All of the entries on your calendar might make it a tad challenging to sit down with your journal for hours on end, contemplating your abundance and saying mantras. Or is it just me?

I didn't think so.

Enter *The Magic Money Minute*, which you can do during any spare moment you have during the day! Just say:

One mantra: such as, *I am a money magnet!*

One intention: such as, *Today IS the best day of my life! Something amazing happens for me today.*

And then you're done! Feel free to put your mantra and intention on a 3 x 5" card from the back of this journal and repeat it all day long, such as:

- Waiting for a green light.
- Washing your hands.
- On hold.
- In line.
- Watching a commercial.
- Sitting down to eat.
  - > And be sure to bless your meal.
- In an elevator
- Getting your mail
- ....Experiencing any other spare moment you have during the day.

Your Magic Money Minutes

One mantra: ______________________________

One intention: ______________________________

One mantra: ______________________________

One intention: ______________________________

One mantra: ______________________________

One intention: ______________________________

One mantra: ______________________________

One intention: ______________________________

One mantra: ______________________________

One intention: ______________________________

One mantra: ______________________________

One intention: ______________________________

One mantra: ______________________________

One intention: ______________________________

One mantra: ______________________________

One intention: ______________________________

One mantra: ______________________________

One intention: ______________________________

INDEX

SAVINGS TRACKER

DATE	AMOUNT SAVED	TOTAL IN SAVINGS	DATE	AMOUNT SAVED	TOTAL IN SAVINGS

DEBT TRACKER

TOTAL DEBT TO PAY OFF:	
AMOUNT PAID	DEBT REMAINING

TOTAL DEBT TO PAY OFF:	
AMOUNT PAID	DEBT REMAINING

MAGIC MONEY MANTRA CARDS

Feel free to cut out these cards and put them in places you'll see them! I've left a couple extra cards for you to create your own. Enjoy!

I am wonderful and I love myself!
This is one of the best days of my life.
Everything is working out for my highest good.
Whatever I need to know is revealed to me.
Whatever I need comes to me.
All is well!

I am a money magnet!
I receive money every day!
I have so much money!

My Magic Money™ Mantra

My Magic Money™ Mantra

My Magic Money™ Mantra

95112793R00152

Made in the USA
Columbia, SC
05 May 2018